100 GREAT HOUSEPLANTS

100 GREAT
HOUSEPLANTS

JOHN EVANS

Photographs by Jacqui Hurst
Illustrations by Sally Maltby

KYLE CATHIE LIMITED

This edition published in Great Britain in 1999 by
Kyle Cathie Limited
20 Vauxhall Bridge Road
London SW1V 2SA

First published in hardback in 1993 and in paperback 1994

10 9 8 7 6 5 4 3 2 1

ISBN 1 85626 3037

Text © 1993 John Evans
Photography © 1993 Jacqui Hurst
Illustration © 1993 Sally Maltby

John Evans is hereby identified as the author of this work in accordance with Section 77 of the Copyright, Designs and Patents Act 1988.

A Cataloguing In Publication record for this title is available from the British Library.

Designed by Geoff Hayes
Cover Design by Button Design Co.

Printed and bound by Sun Fung Offset Binding Co. Ltd.

Acknowledgements

There are a number of people I would like to thank for their work and help on this book.

First, thanks go to Jacqui Hurst for her lovely photographs and Sally Maltby for her beautiful watercolours and line drawings which illustrate the book. A big thank you also to: Susan Haynes and Suellen Dainty for their research; Geoff Hayes for the design of the book; Mrs Peter Bowen, Alison Cathie and Paul Whitfield for opening up their homes to our photographer for the location sections at the front; Marks & Spencer PLC; Floreac, Belgium; Jan Kochem at Lemflora, Denmark; The Royal Horticultural Society; The Garden Centre Association and Chivers Flowers of London. Finally thanks to Kyle Cathie, Caroline Taggart and Beverly Cousins at Kyle Cathie Limited for their hard work, and to all those in my company whom I have pestered from time to time.

Photographs

Grateful acknowledgement is made for permission to reproduce the following photographs: Andrew Lawson, page 24; Boys Syndication, page 12; Eisenbeiss, page 36; Flower Council of Holland, pages 35, 41, 61, 108, 132, 134, 150, 167, 179, 195; Hugh Palmer, pages 18, 19, 25, Mercurius UK Ltd, pages 57, 63, 82, 101, 102, 113, 119, 124, 135, 144, 155, 156, 157, 161, 167, 176, 177, 188, 211, 217, 221; Photo Horticultural, pages 93, 210.

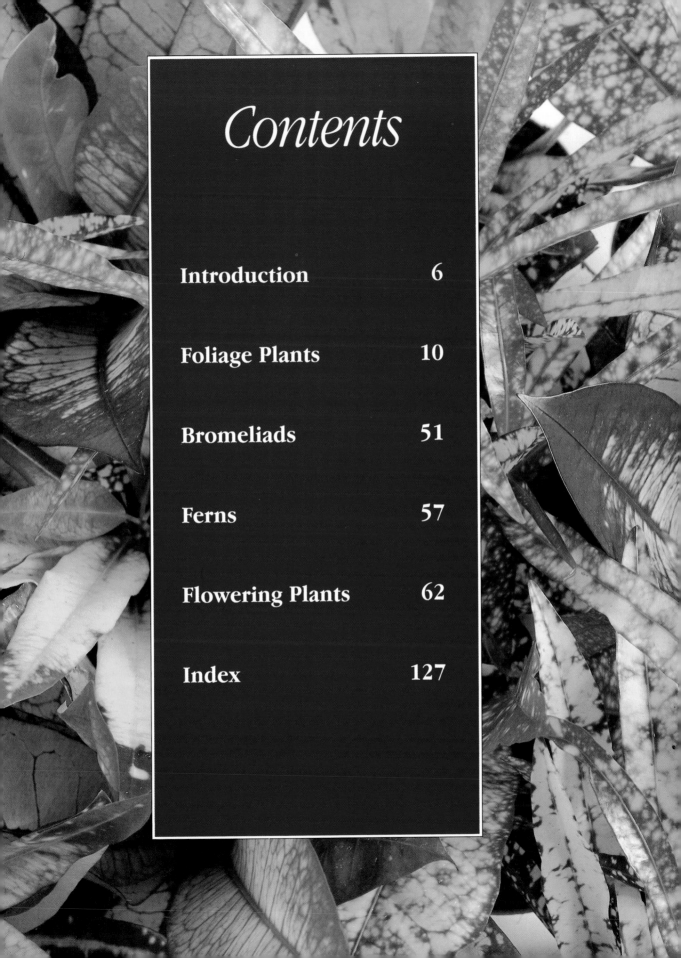

Contents

Introduction

I have been involved with the growing and selling of pot plants all my life. The family business started back in 1876 in south London, moving to Sidcup in the early 1900s and to Ruxley in 1960. We had stands in Covent Garden Market for more than one hundred years, where our plants were sold to the London florists.

In the old days, before my time, the pot plants, loose on shelves, were loaded on to covered carts. Then in the evening driver, horse and cart would slowly wend their way to market. There the plants would be unloaded with the help of porters and set up individually on our stands, ready for my grandfather and his brother to sell them the next morning. I understand there was many a time when the horse found his own way back to the nursery with the driver snoring heavily as a result of a few too many at one of the multitude of ale houses which abounded in the Covent Garden area.

Now we have insulated temperature-controlled vehicles with air suspension. The plants are boxed, care carded, pre-priced, barcoded, sleeved, in fact given state of the art treatment to ensure that they are in peak condition when they reach the retailers' shelves.

Over the last twenty-five years a complete metamorphosis has taken place throughout the indoor plant industry due to a more affluent society, a change in retailing patterns and greatly improved distribution methods. Many books have been written on houseplants, and women's magazines, newspapers and periodicals all have articles on the multitude of species and varieties, which has helped both to popularize plants enormously and to dispel the mystique surrounding the care of plants.

Once upon a time, plants could be bought only at a florist's or at your local nursery. From America in the 1960s came the concept of garden centres. These sprang up in every part of the country and our own at Ruxley Manor was one of the first. Among the many items for sale were houseplants, standing on benches in glasshouse conditions. Never before had plants been sold from conditions similar to those in which they had grown.

Pot plant sales literally took off. From a once fairly limited range available, growers began to seek new plants from Europe and further afield to provide more choice for the customer in the home. The multiples saw their opportunity and Marks and Spencer were the first to sell pot plants in volume in the United Kingdom. But additional demands were then made upon the growers.

RIGHT: *Hedera helix* (ivy) in its variegated form and *Ficus benjamina* (Weeping fig) are two of the most common and versatile indoor plants, easy to grow and long-lasting. Here they are combined with a *begonia rex* and a cyclamen.

Gone were the days of a plant is a plant is a plant. Rigid specifications were placed on every pot: the height, the width, the degree of openness of the flowers, the colour range, the variety to be grown, the hardening off period – all so that the customer would get the best out of the plant once purchased.

This really set the trend for the future of the industry. Allied to the breeding of new varieties, the specialist growers, seed houses and research stations both here and abroad are placing more emphasis on providing plants that will keep better and be more able to cope with the change in conditions from the glasshouse to the home.

Today the glasshouse that produces houseplants is a highly sophisticated place, with computers controlling the heating, watering, lighting and ventilation to very fine limits, so that the plants are able to enjoy near natural conditions. Once in the home, conditions can be very different, but this the grower knows and so makes every effort to acclimatize the plants before they leave the nursery. The industry and the public alike have much to thank Marks and Spencer for.

Today, along with the garden centres, flower shops and market stalls, most multiples the world over sell indoor plants and more people than ever are enjoying the beauty, both in colour and foliage, that plants can bring to the home.

At home, experimentation is vital. How much time are you prepared to devote to caring for your plants? Are you prepared to learn from mistakes? And try again? I was asked to write this book because my editor had failed three times with the same plant, an extremely beautiful new indoor plant adapted from a cut flower. Acknowledging your contribution will direct you into either choosing plants labelled as easy in this book or into tackling the more challenging ones.

The range of pot plants I have chosen should be widely available, as all are grown commercially, though some may only be stocked by the larger garden centres.

Also, I have tried to provide a wide range of foliage plants in varying hues and leaf types, and flowering ones that will follow the seasons covering a wide colour band. After all, plants are like people – different shapes, sizes and colours. And, like people, they all have their aches and pains. Yet they are very adaptable and resilient, though, of course, some are more so than others. There are detailed care instructions about every plant in this book, but basically all that is needed is common sense and consideration for the plant's natural preferences.

Large plants, small plants, hanging plants, and specimen plants – they all have their place, providing the warmth, colour and sheer magic that only they can give.

Easy Care
A long term houseplant which in good conditions will last many years. **Light** *— Bright natural light is best, direct sunlight may scorch leaves, in shade the plant will become spindly. The plant will grow towards the light, turn it occasionally to maintain its shape. Keep away from cold winter draughts.* **Water** *— Water only when the compost is almost dry. Overwatering or standing the pot in water will suffocate the roots and cause the plant to die.* **Feed** *— Weekly April - September with a houseplant fertiliser.* **Other Information** *— Keep leaves dust free, by wiping with a damp cloth, Leafshine can be used on this plant.* **Do not place this container on a polished surface as scratching or staining may occur.**

MARKS & SPENCER PLC
BAKER STREET
LONDON
© 1992
G200

Most plants sold today have care cards giving instructions on how to look after the plant. These instructions range from being thoroughly vague to pertinently precise. Overall the standard has improved greatly and the major multiples and garden centres have gone to great lengths to provide concise information. I have chose the Marks and Spencer 'Easy Care' range as a benchmark.

The care card is split into seven sections, designed to suit all the plants the store sells, and the instructions are really as good as one will ever get on such a small piece of plastic!

An expression such as 'bright natural light, but keep out of direct sun' advises you to keep the plant in a bright area but away from the direct rays of the sun that may come through a window. 'Water only when the compost is almost dry' means water when the compost on the top has dried out.

A specimen plant can be used to great effect in this striking black Victorian fireplace. The blue *Hydrangea* will do fine away from the light it would get near the window for 2 or 3 weeks but should then be moved to a lighter position for the balance of its flowering period

Foliage Plants

There is a rich variety of foliage plants to choose from when decorating your house. The leaf forms and patterns are endless, as this is where photosynthesis and respiration are carried out. On the one hand, there is the enchanting pink and cream colour bands on the delicate green leaves of the *Hypoestes* or the *Tradescantia,* on the other the strongly patterned veins of the *Fittonia* or the *Croton.*

There are plants with delicate and graceful fronds, plants that trail and climb, plants that will reach to the ceiling, plants that will form screens – practically an infinite range.

Whilst the plants in this book are divided into foliage and flowering groups, these divisions are artificial as in the main the foliage plants do flower.

The range of foliage plants marketed has grown vastly since the 1950s, and this book aims to include some of the newer varieties you should look out for.

Aglaonema (Chinese evergreen)

EASY

This group of plants was discovered in the nineteenth century in China and the tropical rainforests and islands of Malaya, Sri Lanka and the Philippines, where they are to be found growing in the shady spots under the tree canopy. There are quite a few varieties, which make good houseplants if kept at a constant temperature and humidity, away from draughts, fires or heaters. They present few problems apart from the occasional yellow leaf if underfed in summer or if allowed to get too cold in winter.

Aglaonema commutatum has decorative variegated foliage – large spear-shaped leaves with silver-green stripes or dots. Sometimes they bloom and, after flowering, develop poisonous red berries.

The plant grows to about 25cm/10in tall and will produce 5–6 new leaves a year. *Aglaonema roebelenii* has thick, leathery, grey-green leaves which grow up to 30cm/1ft long. *Aglaonema crispum* has dark green and silver leaves. The all-green varieties do not require much light, but those with white or variegated yellow foliage need brighter conditions.

The plant will slow down after 2–3 years and should be started again with stem-tip cuttings.

A. roebelenii or
A. crispum
(painted drop tongue)

CARE

Light and temperature
It grows well in constant conditions, without much light, and is fairly tolerant of low temperatures. Ideally temperatures are between 15–24°C/60–75°F – it will withstand 10°C/50°F, but keep the plant on the dry side if the temperature drops this low.

Water and feeding
In summer water thoroughly twice weekly and add liquid fertilizer every 14 days. Do not allow to dry out. Keep much drier in winter. It likes humidity in summer and benefits from spraying twice weekly or being placed over a saucer of wet pebbles. The plant does well in hydroculture.

Propagation
The easiest way to propagate is by division of the root clump. The plant should then be established in a propagator as it will need a high humidity.

Repotting
Repot only as needed, in spring, in a good open compost as the roots like to breathe and good drainage is important.

PROBLEMS

Mealy bug can be a problem, as can red spider mite, if conditions are too light and too dry. Remove them with a cloth soaked in methylated spirit or spray with a systemic insecticide.

Aglaonema commutatum is commonly known as the silver evergreen

Aloe vera (Medicine plant, Barbados aloe, true aloe)

EASY

Aloe vera is sometimes known as *A. barbadensis*

CARE

Light and temperature
Aloe thrives in direct sunlight and a warm temperature, ideally 18°C/64°F. In winter ensure it continues to receive full sunlight and temperatures no lower than 8°C/47°F.

Water and feeding
Immerse the pot in water for 10 minutes, drain well, and allow the compost almost to dry out between waterings. Take care not to let the water settle in the rosette. In winter it will need watering only every 3–4 weeks. Feed monthly in spring and summer with a liquid solution.

Propagation
In spring by removing lateral shoots. The plant yields a sticky pap, so the shoot should be left to dry for 2 days before being planted in a just-damp mixture of no. 2 compost and sand. It should root easily at normal room temperature.

Repotting
Repot young plants annually in spring in a no. 2 potting compost.

PROBLEMS

Take care not to overwater this plant or to let water settle in the rosette as this will cause stem rot, which is recognizable by black marks on the leaves. Allow the compost to dry out completely before watering again and check that the temperature is not too cold.

If the leaves turn brown and dry, the plant has been kept too dry. Soak thoroughly in water for 1 hour and then drain.

If the leaves are a poor colour, the plant does not have enough light. Move to a brighter position.

Aloe vera may be attacked by scale insect. Spray with a systemic insecticide.

This medicinal member of the lily family is a very popular houseplant. Its juice is said to have healing properties for burns, skin and hair, hence its name.

Originally from the semi-arid, subtropical islands of Cape Verde, Canary and Madeira, it is hardy and virtually problem-free. It likes a sunny spot with dry air, the same conditions it enjoys in its native habitat.

Aloe vera grows as a rosette of fleshy, stiff, pointed, grey-green, spotted leaves. It may produce yellow flowers. It is a long-lasting plant and will benefit from a spell outdoors in a sunny, protected spot. There are many new species being marketed.

Anthurium scherzerianum

(Flamingo flower)

Anthurium scherzerianum has a spadix that is twisted spirally

QUITE DIFFICULT

This plant is grown for its decorative heart-shaped leaves and pretty bright red or white oval flowers with creamy-coloured spadix that grow throughout the year.

Originally from Central and South America, as a houseplant it is fairly small, growing to 25cm/10in with a slightly wider spread.

It is not a quick grower, and is not recommended for the beginner. It will need careful monitoring to make sure the conditions are right and must be kept away from draughts and temperature variations. The soil should never be allowed to dry out and a constant humidity level is essential. Mist frequently and stand the pot over damp gravel.

It should last for several years.

CARE

Light and temperature
Strong indirect light and a constant temperature of around 18–21°C/64–70°F is ideal. In winter the temperature should not go below 15°C/60°F.

Water and feeding
Water 2–3 times a week in spring and summer, never allowing the compost to dry out. Stand the pot over damp gravel and mist frequently. In winter, it will need less water. In spring and summer fertilize every 2 weeks with a general houseplant solution.

Propagation
Quite difficult. Divide the plant in late winter, ensuring each section has some roots and stems, and plant in a peat-based compost. Establish at a constant temperature of 21°C/70°F.

Repotting
In spring, every second year, in a peat-based compost.

PROBLEMS

This plant can be quite temperamental as it requires the right conditions in order to thrive. If it is too cold and wet or too dry, the leaves will turn yellow. Check the temperature, watering and humidity levels.

Brown spots on the leaves indicate fungus caused by cold and wet conditions. Spray with a systemic fungicide and check temperature and watering.

Prone to mealy bug, red spider mite and aphids. Remove mealy bug and spider mite with a cloth dipped in methylated spirit and spray aphids with a pyrethrum-based insecticide.

Araucaria heterophylla (Norfolk Island pine)

EASY

Discovered in the South Pacific in 1793 by Captain Cook and Sir Joseph Banks, this handsome pine reaches a height of 60m/200ft in its native habitat. As a houseplant it will grow to a much more manageable 1–1.5m/ 3–6ft. It is a slow grower and after reaching this height is past its best.

The Norfolk Island pine is appealing because of its tiered branches covered with pale green needles. Pruning is not recommended, although this will encourage bushier growth if the plant becomes straggly. The lower branches can be cut off when they become bare.

Araucaria requires a bright, well-lit position, and will enjoy a spell outdoors on mild days. It likes freely circulating air, but not central heating. In summer it needs a lot of moisture, so mist frequently.

Indoors it should last for many years. It can also be used as a Christmas tree.

Araucaria heterophylla has stiff needles, resinous sap and can produce cones

CARE

Light and temperature
A bright, well-ventilated position. In summer it likes temperatures between 18–22°C/64–72°F or a semi-shady spot outdoors with a good breeze. In winter it can withstand cooler temperatures of as low as 5°C/40°F.

Water and feeding
Keep the compost moist in spring, summer and autumn. It will need less water in winter. Mist often. Feed in summer at fortnightly intervals with a general houseplant fertilizer.

Propagation
Difficult to propagate from seed. It is better to buy a small established plant.

Repotting
Repot annually in spring until the plant is 1m/3ft tall, then just replace the topsoil.

PROBLEMS

Dry yellow needles mean conditions are too hot and dry. Water and move to a cooler, well-ventilated spot. Mist frequently.

Mealy bug and greenfly can attack this plant. Treat with a pyrethrum-based insecticide.

Aspidistra (Cast-iron plant)

EASY

Aspidistra comes from China, Japan and the Himalayas, where it grows in poor, marshy soil, and tolerates a range of temperatures, bar frost. It has been a popular houseplant since Victorian times because it flourishes in dark and draughty rooms. It is now enjoying revived popularity because it is attractive, easy to look after and able to withstand most conditions.

A. *elatior* (also known as *A. lurida*) and *A. elatior* 'Variegata' are the most readily available varieties.

It is a slow grower, each year producing only a few elegant, arched, shiny dark green leaves of between 30–46cm/12–18in. Occasionally small purple, bell-shaped flowers will appear at soil level.

Aspidistra will tolerate periods of dryness, but dislikes sunlight, soggy soil and frequent repotting. Clean the leaves with a damp sponge rather than using leaf shine.

Although it is quite expensive, it is virtually an everlasting houseplant.

It will benefit from a spell outdoors in summer.

Aspidistra elatior

A. *elatior* 'Variegata' (variegated cast-iron plant)

The yellow or white striped leaves shoot direct from the rhizome

CARE

Light and temperature
A shady position away from bright light or direct sunlight. *Aspidistra* prefers a cool temperature all year of around 13°C/55°F and as low as 7°C/45°F. It will, however, withstand most temperature fluctuations. Variegated species will need a little more light to maintain the leaf colour.

Water and feeding
Immerse the pot in water for 10 minutes and then drain well. Allow the soil almost to dry out between waterings. Never let the plant stand in water. In winter it will need watering less often, especially if the temperature is below 10°C/50°F. Add liquid food monthly and spray occasionally.

Propagation
Divide into small sections in autumn and place in a good potting mixture, ensuring adequate drainage.

Repotting
The plant does not like to be disturbed too often, so repot every 3 or 4 years in a no. 3 compost, ensuring good drainage.

PROBLEMS

If this plant is subjected to sunlight, brown spots will form on the leaves. Move to a shadier position and cut off the damaged leaves.

Aspidistra is susceptible to scale insect, red spider mite and mealy bug. Treat with a systemic insecticide and improve humidity.

Begonia rex (Leaf begonia)

QUITE EASY

There is an enormous variety of *Begonia rex* hybrids available, and almost all have extremely attractive leaves with beautiful patterns. When choosing, look for good markings and avoid any with damaged leaves or rot on the stem.

Begonia grows in tropical and subtropical areas around the world and specimens from the foothills of the Himalayas were introduced into Europe in Victorian times. It is a most popular houseplant, and will grow to approximately 30cm/12in in height and 46cm/18in in width. It is good as an individual plant or in mixed plantings.

It needs to be kept out of direct sunlight but in a well-lit position and enjoys humidity, but only when the temperature is above 20°C/68°F. It does not like draughts, central heating or varying temperatures.

Begonia leaves are delicate, so treat the plant carefully and do not use leaf shine. Turn the pot regularly to ensure even growth as the plant will tend to grow towards the light.

The plant should last for up to 2 years and is easy to propagate with leaf cuttings.

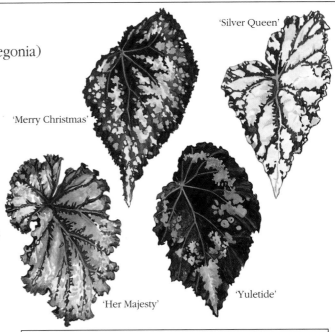

'Silver Queen'

'Merry Christmas'

'Her Majesty'

'Yuletide'

Begonia rex

CARE

Light and temperature
A bright situation but away from direct sunlight. The ideal summer temperature is 21°C/70°F. In winter it can go as low as 10°C/50°F.

Water and feeding
Water twice weekly in summer, with rain water if possible, and spray the leaves regularly. Water only once every 10 days in winter to keep the soil moist. At lower temperatures do not water over the leaves. In spring and summer add liquid fertilizer every 2 weeks.

Propagation
From tip cuttings in late spring. Cut off a shoot below the second pair of leaves. Trim the shoot and remove the lowest pair of leaves. Dip the cut surface in rooting hormone. Insert into compost in a propagator at 21°C/70°F until established.

Repotting
In spring, only when potbound, in a light, open mixture of loam and peat to which a little leaf mould and sand have been added.

PROBLEMS

This is a fragile plant, susceptible to draughts and temperature fluctuations.

If the leaves curl and become brittle, the position is too hot and dry. Water and move to a cooler spot.

If the leaves drop in winter, its position is too cold. Move to a warmer spot.

Red spider mite will cause the leaves to turn dull with webs underneath. Spray with a systemic insecticide.

If there are white or grey powdery patches on the leaves, the plant may have been overwatered and have mildew. Spray with a benomyl-based fungicide and move to a drier area.

Caladium bicolor (Angel wings, mother-in-law plant)

QUITE DIFFICULT

This plant is grown for its distinctive heart-shaped variously coloured leaves which are highlighted with contrasting veins and margins. Originally from Central America and Brazil, in its native tropical habitat *Caladium* grows under shady canopy, as its delicate leaves will burn in direct sunlight.

As a houseplant it should be treated as an annual, except by the expert, as it is very fragile and requires high humidity. The plant produces tubers which can be propagated quite easily.

Caladium grows quickly and may produce a green flower at the end of summer. When the leaves die down in autumn, the compost should be kept just moist and warm. In late winter lay the tubers in a new houseplant mixture, place in a bright spot and keep moist and warm. There are marbled and flecked varieties available.

While growing it likes a bright position out of direct sunlight and away from draughts. It needs plenty of humidity, so stand the pot over damp pebbles and mist frequently. Do not wipe the leaves or use leaf shine. Remove any dead or shrivelled leaves by cutting at the stem base.

Handle this plant carefully as it contains a skin irritant.

CARE

Light and temperature
A bright position, but never direct sunlight. During summer the temperature should be 15–18°C/60–64°F, but can go up to 24°C/75°F if the humidity is increased. In winter, keep the temperature around 13°C/55°F and the compost moist while you are overwintering the tubers.

Water and feeding
Water 2–3 times a week in summer, allowing the compost almost to dry out between waterings. Once the plant has stopped growing, reduce the water gradually until winter when the soil should be kept just moist. Ensure humidity by standing the pot over damp pebbles and spraying with tepid water. Feed with a weak solution of liquid fertilizer every 3 weeks while it is growing.

Propagation
In spring by splitting the overwintered tubers. Establish in a propagator in a mixture of soil, peat and sand at a constant temperature of at least 21°C/70°F.

Repotting
Place tubers in a damp mixture of soil, peat and sand in spring. Keep at a temperature of 24°C/75°F until new leaves appear and mist frequently while the plant becomes established.

PROBLEMS

Greenfly is attracted to this plant. Spray with a systemic insecticide.

Take care not to overwater the plant as this will cause mould on the leaves and the top of the compost. Allow to dry out, ensure there are no draughts and water less often.

The plant needs a certain amount of light to maintain leaf colour. If the leaves fade, conditions are too dark.

Shrivelled leaves mean that the compost is too dry or the temperature too hot. Water immediately and keep the plant moist by standing the pot over damp pebbles and spraying frequently.

Caladium bicolor 'Rhoers Dawn'

Chamaedorea elegans (Parlor palm, good-luck palm)

EASY

This showy, shade-loving miniature is one of the best palms for growing indoors, its small but sturdy stem producing a cluster of dark green pinnate leathery leaves.

Originally from the mountainous forests of Mexico and Guatemala, where it grows as a ground-cover plant under very tall trees, it has been a popular houseplant for more than one hundred years.

Indoors it will take several years to grow to its mature height of 120cm/4ft.

Chamaedorea elegans produces pale yellow, ball-like flowers that turn into berries throughout the year. These flowers should be cut off as soon as they appear so that they do not weaken the plant.

This plant likes to be kept moist and in a shady position although it will cope with dry atmospheres for shortish periods.

Clean the foliage with a damp cloth and spray occasionally with tepid water.

Chamaedorea elegans lives for up to 10 years indoors and 2 or more plants may be stored in the same pot

CARE

Light and temperature
A semi-shady position, near a window, will suit this plant. It likes temperatures of up to 20°C/68°F in summer and no lower than 13°C/55°F in winter.

Water and feeding
Water 2 or 3 times a week, and in spring and summer feed with a weak solution of liquid fertilizer every 2–3 weeks. If conditions are dry, stand the pot over damp pebbles. In winter allow the compost to dry out between waterings.

Propagation
By seed in spring at a high temperature. Its propagation is difficult and best left to a professional.

Repotting
Repot each spring into a pot one size larger using a loam-based compost.

PROBLEMS

Red spider mite may attack the plant in dry and centrally heated air. Treat with a systemic insecticide.

Take care not to overwater the plant, indicated by the leaves turning brown. Allow the compost almost to dry out before watering again. Trim any leaves which have turned brown.

Equally it should not be underwatered or the leaves will turn yellow. Immerse the pot in water for 30 minutes, drain well and mist frequently.

Chlorophytum comosum 'Variegatum'

(Spider plant, airplane plant, St Bernard's lily)

EASY

This rewarding houseplant is graceful, easy and quick to grow (ideal for a beginner), and should last for many years. It is tolerant of most conditions, even occasional neglect, and can be purchased throughout the year.

Originally from the subtropical areas of South Africa, where it grows in semi-shady, rocky outcrops, it was introduced as a houseplant in the mid-nineteenth century.

Chlorophytum has long, narrow, curving bright green leaves with either a cream centre or cream edges. It produces delicate rosettes of white flowers on long stems and these become independent plants with aerial roots that can be potted on. The parent plant will grow up to 46cm/18in in height and width.

Misting should keep the leaves clean as they are too brittle to wipe. Avoid leaf shine.

CARE

Light and temperature
A bright or semi-shady, well-ventilated position, away from direct sunlight, with temperatures not above 18°C/64°F in summer or below freezing point in winter. It can tolerate dark places, although leaves are more strongly coloured with bright light.

Water and feeding
Water 2–3 times a week in summer, allowing the soil almost to dry out between waterings, and once a week in winter. Mist daily. Add liquid food to the water every 2 weeks in summer.

Propagation
Roots and stems can be divided, the old soil carefully removed and smaller plants repotted. As the plantlets produce roots, these can be potted on in a small pot beside the parent. When established with new leaves of their own, these plantlets can be cut away from the parent. Alternatively, plantlets can be rooted in water and then potted at any time during the year.

Repotting
Chlorophytum is quite a quick grower and you may need to repot the parent plant twice a year. Use a loam-based mixture, and try not to break the roots when handling the plant.

PROBLEMS

If the plant is looking out of sorts, it may need feeding or is too warm.

Chlorophytum is sensitive to overwatering. If there are brown, slimy marks in the centre of the plant, allow the compost to dry out more between waterings.

The plant also needs plenty of humidity in the form of daily misting or the leaf tips will turn brown or become shrivelled. These tips can be cut off but will go brown again after a few weeks.

Dry air will also attract red spider mite and aphids. Treat spider mite with a systemic insecticide and aphids with pyrethrum-based insecticide.

Chrysalidocarpus lutescens

QUITE DIFFICULT   (Areca palm, yellow palm, butterfly palm)

This slow-growing member of the palm family has graceful yellow-green pinnate fronds of up to 60cm/2ft long and 1.5cm/½in across which curve from a number of slender yellowish stems.

Originally from Madagascar, and bought commercially from Florida, *Chrysalidocarpus* needs bright but indirect light and warmish, humid conditions. It can withstand cool temperatures, but this will hinder growth. Avoid dry air and mist frequently. It does well in a conservatory.

As a houseplant, in the right conditions, it can grow 20cm/8in a year, reaching 2m/6ft as a mature plant. It should last for many years.

CARE

Light and temperature
Good light, but never direct sunlight. It enjoys a warm temperature of between 18–22°C/ 64–71°F all year round with a maximum of 27°C/80°F in summer and a minimum of 10°C/50°F in winter.

Water and feeding
Water thoroughly, but do not allow the compost to become saturated or to dry out. Feed with a liquid solution every 2 weeks in spring and summer.

Propagation
In spring by seed in a propagator with a constant temperature of 18–20°C/64–68°F. Alternatively, remove basal shoots with some roots and place in a mixture of soil, peat and sand. Cover with plastic and leave in a bright position until established.

Repotting
Repot in spring, only as needed, in the mixture recommended above.

PROBLEMS

Scale insect and red spider mite can attack this plant. Spray with a systemic insecticide and increase humidity by misting frequently.

If the air is too dry the leaves will turn yellow or develop brown spots. Improve moisture and humidity. Remove damaged leaves.

Chrysalidocarpus lutescens produces many suckers at the base of the plant, which can be separated and potted up

Cissus antarctica (Kangaroo vine, kangaroo ivy)

EASY

Cissus antarctica is a quick-growing climber, particularly useful for covering large areas quickly. It also looks good in a hanging basket.

This plant comes from Australia where it grows naturally among the protected undergrowth of the bush in the subtropical areas of New South Wales. As a houseplant it likes a cool position with plenty of water in summer and regular misting to prevent the leaves from turning brown at the edges.

Cissus antarctica has a dense, shrubby base with tendrils that grow to about 3m/9ft in length, which grip easily on to a trellis. It has glossy green oval leaves with brown veins and serrated edges. It is a good idea to pinch out new growth occasionally to encourage a dense plant, though it can easily be pruned back if it does become straggly.

The leaves should be cleaned occasionally with rain water. Do not use leaf shine.

Other popular members of the *Cissus* family are the delicately leaved *C. striata* and the interestingly variegated *C. discolor.*

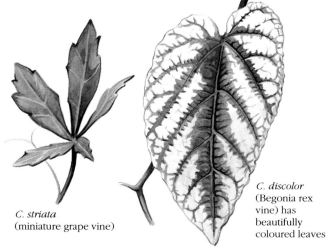

C. striata
(miniature grape vine)

C. discolor
(Begonia rex vine) has beautifully coloured leaves

CARE

Light and temperature
Keep *Cissus antarctica* in strong but indirect light. The ideal summer temperature is 18–21°C/64–70°F, and in winter no lower than 12°C/54°F.

Water and feeding
Water 2–3 times a week in summer, allowing the compost almost to dry out between waterings. In winter keep the compost just moist and water only every 2 weeks. Add a little liquid fertilizer at fortnightly intervals in summer.

Propagation
In spring using stem-tip cuttings with new growth which will root easily in a mixture of compost and sand. Cover the pot with plastic and put in a warm spot with suffused light until the new plants become established.

Repotting
If the plant is growing vigorously you may need to repot it twice a year. Once it reaches the desired height you can keep it in the same pot and just change the topsoil in spring.

PROBLEMS

If webs appear on the underside of the leaves the plant has been attacked by red spider mite. Spray with systemic insecticide and improve humidity.

Greenfly will cause the leaves to become distorted. Spray with a pyrethrum-based insecticide.

Brown or brittle leaves mean that the plant is too dry and hot. Water and mist well and move to a cooler position.

Take care not to overwater the plant or the leaves will develop brown spots and become mildewy. Check that the drainage is adequate and allow the compost to dry out between waterings. Mildew can be treated with a benomyl-based fungicide.

Cissus antarctica 'Ellen Danica'

Codiaeum (Joseph's coat)

QUITE DIFFICULT

Originally from the tropical areas of Malaysia and Indonesia, this most colourful but fragile houseplant has been popular since it was introduced in the mid-nineteenth century.

Its smooth, laurel-shaped, variegated leaves range in colour from green to yellow, orange and red, with mottled or striped yellow markings. It can grow into quite a large shrub, around 1m/3ft tall and across.

Codiaeum requires constant humid conditions, away from draughts and central heating. Strong light is needed to maintain colour in the leaves; however the plant should not be sprayed while it is in sunlight or the leaves will burn.

The plant rests in winter and loses many of its bottom leaves, so it is often treated as an annual, though the experienced grower can expect it to live for many years and can ensure a bushy plant by removing the growing tips.

Codiaeum 'Gold King'

'Excellent'

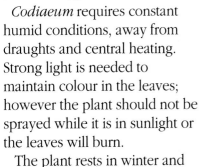

'Norma'

'Mrs Iceton'

CARE

Light and temperature
Bright, and occasionally direct, sunlight and a constant temperature all year no lower than 16°C/61°F.

Water and feeding
In summer water 2–3 times a week. Take care never to let the plant dry out. In winter use tepid water every 4–5 days. Spray occasionally to provide humidity and keep the leaves clean. Stand the pot over damp gravel. Feed with a liquid fertilizer every 2 weeks in summer.

Propagation
In spring by stem-tip cuttings using a propagator at a temperature of about 24°C/75°F. The plant yields a milky juice so sprinkle the cuttings in charcoal powder to seal the 'wound' before planting. Use gloves while handling the plant as the juice contains an irritant.

Repotting
In late spring, annually or as needed, in a loam-based compost. Pack tightly, but ensure good drainage.

PROBLEMS

Prone to red spider mite. Spray with a systemic insecticide and improve humidity. Also scale insect and mealy bug. Remove these with a cloth dipped in methylated spirit.

If the bottom leaves drop off, the conditions are too dry or cold or fluctuating. Move to a warmer spot where the conditions are more easily controllable.

Brown tips and shrivelled leaves are caused by hot, dry air or underwatering. Immerse the pot in water for 10 minutes, drain well, and do not allow the compost to dry out. Improve humidity by standing the pot over damp gravel and spraying frequently. The plant may also need to be moved to a cooler position. Damaged leaves can be cut off.

Overwatering will cause stem rot, recognizable by brown patches on the stem and a drooping of the leaves. Allow the compost to dry out and water less.

Coleus blumei (Flame nettle)

EASY

This cultivated hybrid is grown for its highly coloured leaves. If the growing tips are pinched out regularly it should become an attractive, bushy plant of 60cm/2ft. It was introduced from Java in 1853.

Indoors it is often grown as an annual because it is quick-growing and easy to propagate. If the plant becomes very tired in winter and you wish to keep it rather than propagate, it can be cut back in spring to within 7.5cm/3in of the compost. *Coleus blumei* likes a moist atmosphere and needs direct light to keep its colours strong and its foliage in good condition.

Coleus blumei

Four of the numerous *Coleus blumei* hybrids

CARE

Light and temperature
Bright, direct sunlight with a warm temperature, ideally around 21°C/70°F. It will withstand temperatures of around 10°C/50°F, but likes slightly higher, preferably not below 13°C/55°F.

Water and feeding
Coleus needs moist, humid conditions so the soil should always be kept damp and the pot stood over wet gravel. Mist often. Keep the compost drier in winter. Feed with a liquid solution every 2 weeks, except in winter.

Propagation
Cut the plant back during winter and keep the compost quite dry. In early spring encourage new growth by watering and fertilizing. Take tip cuttings and place in a damp no. 1 compost. Keep in a shady spot at a temperature of 18°C/64°F.

Repotting
Repot in summertime as the plant outgrows its pot. To check this, remove the plant from the pot and see if it is rootbound.

PROBLEMS

If the temperature is too cool or there is insufficient water or moisture the plant will lose its leaves.

Prone to red spider mite in dry conditions. Remove individually with a cloth soaked in methylated spirit and improve humidity.

Ctenanthe oppenheimiana

QUITE DIFFICULT   (Never-never plant)

This Brazilian plant is much sought after for the unusual dark green markings on its pale green foliage. An attractive plant, it has long stalks that produce large pointed elliptical leaves of up to 30cm/12in long which are red underneath.

   Its native habitat is the Alto de Sena region in South East Brazil, which has 350–400cm/140–160in of rain per year. It grows along the escarpments of this wet coastal range and is found underneath the low tree canopy of these dripping forests.

   Ctenanthe is a good houseplant because it enjoys average room temperatures and has no particular needs. As long as it is not overwatered and has adequate humidity in the form of misting and standing the pot over damp gravel, it should do well. Indoors it should grow to 1m/3ft high and wide.

   The plant has a dormant period in winter when it will simply need to be kept warm and the compost prevented from drying out.

   It should last for 5–6 years, becoming an attractively bushy plant.

CARE

Light and temperature
Semi-shade during summer at 18–21°C/64–70°F, but it will accept temperatures up to 29°C/85°F. In winter it prefers more light and will withstand temperatures as low as 10°C/50°F if kept almost dry.

Water and feeding
Water thoroughly in spring and summer. Place the pot over pebbles almost covered with water as this plant enjoys high humidity coupled with warm temperatures. Spray daily. Feed every 2 weeks with general houseplant fertilizer from early spring to end of summer. During winter water once a week and less if the temperature drops to 10°C/50°F.

Propagation
In spring from stem cuttings with several leaves. Treat with a rooting powder and pot in a mixture of peat and sand. Cover with plastic or place in a greenhouse at 21°C/70°F until established.

Repotting
In spring in a no. 2 peat-based compost.

PROBLEMS

Mealy bug, scale insect and red spider mite can attack this plant. Spray mealy bug with diluted malathion and scale insect and spider mite with a systemic insecticide.

Hot, dry conditions will cause the leaves to curl. Water well and increase humidity by misting and standing the pot over damp gravel.

If the position is too cold in winter the plant will suffer root rot. Allow to dry out, water less frequently and move to a warmer position.

Ctenanthe lubbersiana has a more upright habit than *C.O. tricolor*

Dieffenbachia (Dumb cane, leopard lily)

Dieffenbachia picta 'Marianne' is one of the spotted dumb canes

QUITE DIFFICULT

This ornamental houseplant originally came from the tropical rain forests of Colombia, Costa Rica and Venezuela. Growing from a thick stem are elongated dark green leaves which are attractively variegated with creamy yellow in the centre.

As a houseplant it grows up to 1m/3ft. It is a quick grower and can last for a long time, though as the plant becomes older it sheds its lower leaves and is best replaced after 3–4 years.

It requires constant and warm conditions, like those it enjoys in its native habitat, and will do well in central heating as long as it is misted daily and the pot stood over damp gravel. It also benefits from a spell outdoors in summer in a shady spot. It does not like draughts, so make sure it is placed in a protected position.

Dieffenbachia produces a poisonous sap, so always wear gloves when handling the plant.

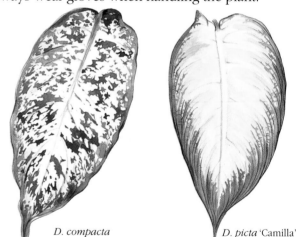

D. compacta   *D. picta* 'Camilla'

CARE

Light and temperature
This plant thrives in a shady position with a little indirect light. The ideal temperature is around 18°C/64°F. If above 20°C/70°F it will need even more humidity. Do not let the temperature go below 10°C/50°F.

Water and feeding
Water well in summer, probably every second day, as the compost must always be kept moist, but never soggy. In winter water less as the plant will not be growing and soil should be allowed almost to dry out between waterings. Feed every 2 weeks in summer with a liquid fertilizer.

Propagation
By stem-tip cuttings just below a node. Treat the base with a rooting powder and bury the cuttings in a pot filled with damp peat and sand. Place in a greenhouse or wrap in plastic and keep in bright light at a constant temperature of 21–24°C/70–75°F until established. It can also be propagated by cutting the stem into 7–8cm/3in sections and burying in the same medium.

Repotting
In spring, in a mixture of organic soil, peat and sand.

PROBLEMS

Prone to stem rot, indicated by a slimy stem. Do not allow the plant to get too wet. Dust damaged areas with sulphur and take care not to overwater.

Overwatering will also cause the leaves to turn yellow. Allow the compost to dry out and water less.

If the lower leaves droop, the position is too cold. Move to a warmer spot.

Epipremnum aureum (Devil's ivy)

EASY

This plant is also commonly known as *Scindapsus aureus*.
A vigorous climber, it comes from the humid tropical Solomon and South East Asian islands, where it attaches itself to the bark of host tree trunks.

It is easy to grow indoors and as a houseplant its aerial roots can be trained to cover a moss pole to a height of 1–1.5m/3–5ft, or its tendrils can look good trailing over a hanging basket. The plant can also be grown in water.

Epipremnum has glossy green leaves covered with yellow patches or spots. These will gradually fade and should be removed from the stem. Pinch out new shoots occasionally to ensure dense growth. It needs warm, humid conditions and should be sprayed frequently with tepid water.

Wash your hands after handling the plant as the leaves contain an irritant.

Epipremnum aureum
'Marble Queen'

Epipremnum aureum

CARE

Light and temperature
Bright indirect light with temperatures around 18–24°C/64–75°F all year, and never below 13°C/55°F.

Water and feeding
In spring and summer water 2–3 times a week, allowing the soil to dry out between waterings. Good drainage is essential for this plant. Water less in winter. Spray frequently. Use a liquid fertilizer every 2 weeks in spring and summer.

Propagation
In spring from stem-tip cuttings 10cm/4in long. Allow to root in water and then plant in the mixture recommended below.

Repotting
Every other year in a peat-based no. 2 compost.

PROBLEMS

Ensure good drainage and avoid overwatering as the plant can develop stem rot. Allow the compost to dry out and water less frequently.

If the position is too damp or dark there may be root rot and leaf drop. Move to a brighter position.

White woolly patches on the leaves indicate mealy bug. Remove with a cloth dipped in methylated spirit or spray with diluted malathion.

Ficus benjamina 'Starlight' (Weeping fig)

EASY

This relatively recent introduction from Israel is a very much improved version of *Ficus benjamina* 'Variegata', the much sought-after tropical tree also known as the 'weeping fig'.

In good conditions 'Starlight' will grow to a densely foliaged 3m/9ft, its leaves very much whiter than the original plant and dappled with green blotches.

As a houseplant it should last for many years.

CARE

Light and temperature
Being variegated it is important that it is in a very good light situation, but away from the midday sun where the leaves could burn. It enjoys temperatures up to 24°C/75°F in summer and no lower than 13°C/55°F in winter.

Water and feeding
Water thoroughly in spring and summer, but allow the surface of the compost to dry out between waterings. Do not let the plant stand in water or the leaves will drop. During summer spray daily, particularly during high temperatures. Feed at fortnightly intervals during spring and summer with a general houseplant liquid fertilizer. In winter, depending on the temperature, 1 good watering per week should suffice.

Propagation
By stem-tip cuttings taken in spring and placed in a compost of peat and sand and maintained in a propagator at 24°C/75°F. Water the cuttings thoroughly.

Repotting
Annually in spring into a no. 2 peat-based compost. When the plant is mature, you will only need to change the topsoil in the container.

Opposite: *Ficus benjamina* 'Starlight'

PROBLEMS

If the leaves drip, the plant is receiving insufficient light or too much water.

Brown scaly insects on the underside of the leaves will cause leaf discoloration. Remove the insects with a cloth dipped in methylated spirit.

Cobwebs on the underside of the leaves indicates red spider mite. Spray with a systemic insecticide, check watering and spray more often.

F. nitida (Indian laurel) is a sun-lover and greedy for light. Its leaves are a rich dark green and the plant has an erect habit. It is used as an outdoor tub plant in the southwest of America. It does well, even in dry atmospheres.

F. 'Curly' is a colourful variety of weeping fig. Keep it in a very light position so that the leaves are well variegated.

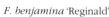

F. longifolium likes similar conditions to *F. benjamina* but has elongated dark green leaves of up to 14cm/6in; they look dramatic displayed against white walls.

F. benjamina 'Natasha'

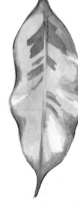

F. benjamina 'Reginald'

Ficus elastica robusta (Indian rubber plant)

EASY

This sturdy old favourite with glossy, deep green foliage is possibly the most common houseplant of all.

Originally from the moist tropical areas of India and Malaysia, where it grows as a large tree up to 30m/90ft in height, this relatively new commercial variety is an improved version of the original, *Ficus decora*.

It is easy to grow, but is susceptible to root rot if its soil is allowed to become soggy, so take care not to overwater it.

Ficus elastica robusta can grow up to 10m/30ft indoors in a warm situation with good light. It will live to a ripe old age and can acclimatize itself to a wide range of conditions. But do remember to keep it out of dark corners and draughts.

To develop a strong, bushy plant pinch out the growing tips occasionally. The plant will 'bleed' a white sticky substance when cut, so seal the wound with petroleum jelly.

CARE

Light and temperature
Bright conditions with some direct sunlight each day. It prefers a minimum temperature of 13°C/55°F throughout the year.

Water and feeding
Water thoroughly but allow the compost to dry out between waterings. Rain water is recommended since tap water may cause lime deposits on the roots which slows down the growth. Never allow the plant to stand in water for more than an hour. In winter water once a week at the most – the lower the temperature the less water is required. Feed weekly with a liquid fertilizer in spring and summer.

Propagation
Take a 7.5cm/3in length of fleshy, not woody, stem with a leaf attached. Treat it with a rooting hormone and provide bottom heat while the new plant becomes established.

Repotting
Once a year in spring in a no. 2 compost. The plant needs a large pot and probably a stake to keep it stable. For mature plants it is only necessary to change the topsoil in the pot.

PROBLEMS

If root rot occurs, indicated by leaf drop and a straggly plant, treat it immediately by completely removing the soggy compost to expose the roots. Cut away the infected roots and dust with charcoal. Repot in fresh compost.

Brown areas on the leaves mean the plant has been scorched by the sun or is too close to a heater.

Scale insect and red spider mite can attack this plant. Treat with systemic insecticide.

Ficus elastica robusta

Ficus pumila (Creeping fig)

QUITE EASY

An elegant creeper which can also be kept in a hanging basket or trained to grow up a moss-covered pole.

Originally from the temperate areas of Indo-China and Japan, where it grows like ivy climbing over walls, *Ficus pumila* has a many-branched stem and thin, slightly crinkled, heart-shaped, dark green leaves which become larger and more oblong as the plant matures. It should grow several trails a year. There are variegated varieties, such as 'Sonny' and 'Bellis'.

This plant withstands quite cool temperatures and likes a rest period in winter at 7–10°C/44–50°F. Spray daily in summer and every second day in winter (daily if it is in a centrally heated room). This should also keep the leaves clean. Do not use leaf shine.

Ficus pumila is a long-living plant provided it is kept moist and humid, but never soggy. Cut back occasionally to encourage a dense and bushy plant.

CARE

Light and temperature
Good indirect light and a warm, shady position. In summer it will tolerate up to 30°C/84°F but the plant requires plenty of humidity at this temperature. Spray frequently. It will withstand a temperature as low as 6°C/43°F in winter as long as it is kept very much on the dry side.

Water and feeding
Water carefully, allowing the top of the compost to dry out between waterings. Never let it dry out completely, even in winter, or become soggy. Mist often. Feed every 2 weeks in spring and summer with a liquid fertilizer.

Propagation
In spring with stem-tip cuttings potted in a mixture of peat and sand. Remove lower leaves, cover with plastic and place in indirect light until new shoots appear. Repot after 4 months.

Repotting
In spring as necessary in a good house-plant mixture.

PROBLEMS

If the leaves fall off, the plant has either been allowed to dry out or its winter position is too cool and damp.

Scale insect and red spider mite may attack this plant. Spray with a systemic insecticide and improve humidity.

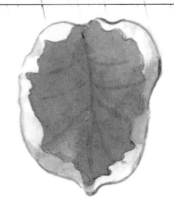

'Bellis'

'Sonny'

Ficus pumila

Fittonia (Snakeskin plant, mosaic plant, painted net leaf, silver net leaf)

DIFFICULT

This pretty foliage plant has delicate veined oval leaves about 7.5cm/3in long. There are two varieties: *F. argyroneura*, which has olive-green leaves with a distinct white veining, and *F. verschaffeltii*, with slightly darker green leaves and a red veining. There are also miniature versions of each. Green flowers may appear in summer and should be cut off immediately so as not to impede the plant's growth.

Originally from the tropical rainforests of Peru, where it grows as a low ground-cover creeper, it was introduced as a houseplant in the mid-nineteenth century.

Fittonia is an attractive and popular specimen that flourishes in shady situations, but it is quite difficult to grow because it needs a constant, humid temperature never below 18°C/64°F. Draughts, dry air and direct sunlight must be avoided at all costs. The plant is ideal in bottle gardens and terrariums and good in mixed bowls.

Fittonia tends to become straggly, so the new growth should be pinched out regularly to encourage density.

For the expert, this plant will have a long life.

F. verschaffeltii
(painted net leaf)

CARE

Light and temperature
A bright to semi-shady position, but no direct sunlight. A warm temperature all year, never below 18°C/64°F.

Water and feeding
Keep the compost damp but never soggy using tepid water. Dry air will kill the plant so mist often and stand the pot over wet gravel or surround with damp peat. Feed monthly in summer with a liquid fertilizer.

Propagation
In spring using stem-tip cuttings. They will need to be established in a heated propagator at around 24°C/75°F.

Repotting
Annually in spring, in a half pot as the plant has a very shallow root system. Use a no. 2 potting compost or a no. 2 peat-based compost.

PROBLEMS

Draughts or a cold surrounding temperature will cause the leaves to drop. Move to a warmer, more protected position and improve humidity.

Dry air and direct sunlight will cause shrivelled leaves. Soak the plant in water for 30 minutes, drain well and place in a semi-shady position. Never let the compost dry out.

Yellow leaves are caused by overwatering. Remove the damaged leaves, check the drainage and allow the compost almost to dry out before watering again. Water less often.

Greenfly can attack this plant. Spray with a systemic insecticide.

Fittonia argyroneura nana (silver net leaf)

Hedera canariensis (Canary Islands ivy)

EASY

This is one of the most popular varieties of ivy for the house. It is tolerant of most conditions and is easy to grow – an ideal plant for a beginner and the neglectful.

A native of the Canary Islands, where it grows freely on lower slopes, it has largish, slightly leathery, all-green leaves, but there are variegated varieties available which have silver, grey or white markings. The variety 'Gloire de Marengo' is recommended.

H. canariensis is long-lasting and a fairly quick grower that will attach itself easily to a stake, pillar or wall. It can also be grown outdoors if it is not too cold. If you do move the plant outside, do so in summer to allow it to establish itself before winter.

Pinch out the growing tips regularly to encourage a dense and bushy specimen.

Regular spraying should keep the leaves clean; if not, wipe with a damp cloth. Do not use leaf shine.

As a houseplant, it likes cool, humid conditions and will not do well if it is too hot or dry. Also take care not to overwater this plant.

CARE

Light and temperature
Bright light is essential, especially for a variegated plant. It can tolerate most temperatures, but prefers to be kept cool, the ideal being between 7–15°C/45–60°F. If the temperature is warmer, increase the humidity.

Water and feeding
Water once or twice a week in spring and summer and less in winter. Mist frequently for humidity and stand the pot over damp pebbles. In summer feed fortnightly with a liquid fertilizer.

Propagation
By stem-tip cuttings which are most easily rooted in water. Plant 2 or 3 together when established.

Repotting
Repot younger plants in spring. If the plant is growing vigorously, you may need to do this twice a year. For mature plants it is only necessary to change the topsoil.

PROBLEMS

The edges of the leaves will turn brown if the position is too dry or hot. Move to a cooler spot and improve humidity.

Black spots on the leaves mean that the plant has been overwatered. Allow to dry out and water less.

Prone to red spider mite and greenfly. Spray with a systemic insecticide and improve the humidity level.

Thrip can be sprayed with a pyrethrum-based insecticide.

Scale insect will discolour the leaves. Remove with a cloth dipped in methylated spirit.

Hedera canariensis 'Gloire de Marengo' has been cultivated in Europe for over 200 years

Hedera helix (Common ivy, English ivy)

EASY

In ancient times ivy was the plant associated with Bacchus, the god of wine. Today there are many varieties available, but *Hedera helix* is among the most popular, as it is a quick grower and will cling easily to almost all surfaces. It also looks good in a hanging basket or as a standard.

Hedera helix grows freely in Europe, Asia and North Africa. Its lobed leaves are a glossy dark green with cream veins, growing up to 6cm/2in long.

Ivy is quite difficult to cultivate indoors because it likes a cool temperature and does not fare well in a centrally heated room. It will need frequent misting to ensure adequate humidity.

The plant will soon become straggly unless new growth is regularly pinched out. These cuttings can be propagated.

Hedera helix will have a long life, and can be moved outdoors where it will continue to grow well albeit more slowly.

Hedera helix 'Golden Child'

CARE

Light and temperature
Bright to semi-shady conditions. Variegated plants will need light to maintain leaf colour. The temperature should be cool, ideally 15°C/60°F, and preferably unheated in winter.

Water and feeding
Do not overwater – 2–3 times a week should be sufficient in summer to keep the compost moist. In winter water less, although if it is in a heated room it will need more watering and misting. Wipe the leaves occasionally with a damp cloth. In summer feed every 2 weeks with a liquid solution.

Propagation
Easily done from stem tips or aerial roots which root easily in water or a potting mixture.

Repotting
In spring every 2 years in a good houseplant mixture. Cut the plant back at the same time to encourage bushiness.

PROBLEMS

If the plant is located in a dry position, the leaf tips will turn brown and attract spider mite and scale insect. Treat with a systemic insecticide and mist frequently to improve humidity.

If the leaf edges are brown, conditions are too warm. Cut back and move to a cooler spot.

If the veining becomes slight move to a brighter position.

Fine holes in the leaves may indicate that the plant is infested with thrips. Treat with a pyrethrum-based insecticide.

Howea <small>(Paradise palm, kentia palm, sentry palm)</small>

QUITE DIFFICULT

This palm is native to Lord Howe Island off the east coast of Australia, where it lives in subtropical, seaside conditions. It has only recently become a sought-after houseplant.

The differences between the two species – *H. forsteriana* (paradise palm or kentia palm) and *H. belmoreana* (sentry palm) – are sometimes hard to distinguish. In its native habitat, *H. forsteriana* will grow up to 20m/60ft, its fronds well spaced and durable. *H. belmoreana* is more slow-growing and its fronds are thinner and more upright.

Both varieties have a single, robust trunk from which grow dark green pinnate fronds which should be cleaned regularly with a damp cloth. The plants may also produce clusters of yellow-green fruit.

Avoid direct sunlight which will turn the leaf tips brown. *Howea* can withstand almost completely shady conditions, but the plant will not grow unless there is some light. Good drainage is essential.

Howea is extremely long-lasting – up to 80 years.

PROBLEMS

Howea adapts well as a houseplant as long as it has a warm, humid and protected spot and is neither overwatered nor underwatered.

Overwatering will make the leaves turn brown. Allow to dry out and water less.

Underwatering will make the leaves turn yellow. Immerse the pot in water for 30 minutes, drain well, and never allow the compost to dry out.

The lower leaves will die naturally, and should be cut off.

Red spider mite will attack the plant if conditions are too dry. Spray with a systemic insecticide and improve humidity.

Howea forsteriana

Hypoestes sanguinolenta (Polka dot plant, freckle face)

QUITE DIFFICULT

Clockwise from the top: *H. s.* 'Bettina', *H. s.* 'Rose', *H. s.* 'White', *H. s.* 'Ruby'

A showy houseplant originating from Madagascar, where it grows in humid, tropical conditions as a ground-cover plant. It has small, downy, oblong green leaves with coloured veins and splashes of pink spots. New varieties have been bred to include white, ruby and rose colourings and these are much more compact in habit. There are often several plants in a small pot.

Hypoestes is a very good ground-cover plant for mixed bowls and bottle gardens, but it needs adequate light to keep its colouring bright and vibrant. It also tends to become very straggly and it is best to replace it annually. Pinch out the growing tips in young plants.

This plant is quite particular about its position. Do not put it in a dry atmosphere or near a heater or gas fire. Do not use leaf shine.

CARE

Light and temperature
It likes bright, indirect sunlight, with plenty of warmth and humidity. Place the pot over damp pebbles and maintain a temperature of 18–24°C/64–75°F all year round if possible.

Water and feeding
Water 2–3 times a week in summer, and possibly only once a week in winter using tepid water. Feed with half the recommended dose of liquid fertilizer at fortnightly intervals.

Propagation
It is best to raise a new plant from seed each spring. Cuttings can also be rooted in spring and summer in a mixture of soil, peat and sand. Either place them in a propagator or cover the pot with plastic and keep at a constant temperature of not less than 21°C/70°F while they become established.

Repotting
If growing fast, pot on during the first season. Discard when plant becomes leggy.

PROBLEMS

This plant is sensitive to the cold and to being overwatered in winter, causing it to droop. Allow the soil to dry out in a warmer position and then water less.

Discoloured leaves indicate the plant has been attacked by scale insect. Remove these with a cloth dipped in methylated spirit.

Maranta leuconeura (Prayer plant, rabbit's tracks, red herringbone plant)

QUITE DIFFICULT

M. l. 'Kerchoveana' and *M. l.* 'Erythrophylla' (also known as *M. tricolor*) are two of the most popular varieties of this family of plants renowned for its beautiful leaf markings, some almost appearing as if they are hand-painted.

Both are known as prayer plants as their leaves curl up at night.

Maranta is quite a difficult houseplant to maintain because of its humidity requirements, but worth persevering with. It should last for many years, but it is usually best to divide the plant after 3 or 4 years.

Originally from the tropical rainforests of South America, where it grows as a small plant with spreading branches under the protection of the tree canopy, *Maranta* likes warm conditions with plenty of humidity. Use soft and tepid water at all times. Spray daily and stand the pot on wet pebbles or surround with moist peat to ensure good humidity. If spraying doesn't keep the leaves clean, wipe gently with a damp cloth. Do not use leaf shine.

'Amabilis'

'Freddy'

M. ornata

CARE

Light and temperature
Bright light but never direct sun. It likes warm temperatures, ideally 16–18°C/60–64°F all year, and as high as 28°C/83°F if there is good humidity. Avoid draughts.

Water and feeding
Keep the compost moist at all times with tepid water, never allowing it to dry out between waterings. It will need less water in winter. Mist leaves regularly. Feed every 2 weeks in late spring and early summer with a weak liquid solution.

Propagation
Divide the plant in early spring as new growth emerges, ensuring each division has both roots and stems, and transfer to individual 9cm/4in pots. Cover with plastic and keep warm – 18°C/64°F – until established.

Repotting
In spring every 2–3 years in a peat-based compost. Ensure adequate drainage.

PROBLEMS

This is a delicate plant. Falling leaves or brown leaf tips may be caused by the air being too dry. Remove dead growth and improve the humidity. Also check for red spider mite and remove with a cloth dipped in methylated spirit.

Underwatering is indicated by curled or spotted leaves and yellow lower leaves. Remove the damaged leaves and keep the compost moist at all times.

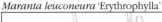

Maranta leuconeura 'Erythrophylla'

Philodendron

EASY

The *Philodendron* family is versatile and far ranging. Few of the many trailing and climbing species will present problems either for the beginner or for the neglectful plant owner.

Until the beginning of the twentieth century, philodendrons were unknown outside their native habitat of tropical South America. There, the plants scramble over tree trunks in dense jungle, their roots attaching themselves to the tree bark. The plants bloom wonderfully here, but it is rare for the indoor philodendron to produce a decent flower. On average you can expect a lifespan of 5 years.

Philodendron scandens (the sweetheart plant, parlour ivy or heart-leafed philodendron) is an easy and popular small-leafed species. Its constant growth and glossy, waxy leaves make it a durable indoor plant in a group arrangement. It will climb willingly, and is particularly suited to moss-covered supports. Equally it can be used effectively in hanging basket arrangements.

Pinch out the growing shoots regularly to keep the bushy shape of the plant.

CARE

Light and temperature
Some, like *P. scandens*, will grow happily in shade. Most, however, like bright light. Average warmth, with temperatures not less than 12–18°C/55–64°F in winter, and not more than 24°C/75°F in summer. High humidity is important so if possible stand plants on a tray of moist pebbles.

Watering and feeding
Water twice weekly during summer, once a week during winter. Spray the leaves with tepid rain water to help humidity. A weak solution of liquid food should be added to the watering once a fortnight during the summer months.

Repotting
Only when the plant becomes top-heavy. Once the plant has matured, in an 18cm/7in pot, just change the topsoil each spring. If the leaves look poor and growth is not apparent repot in spring.

Propagation
Not easy, as they are normally propagated from seed grown in the tropics. Stem cuttings can be taken, but again not easy. Try in early summer: dip in rooting hormone powder and then into fresh compost at a temperature of 24°C/75°F.

P. melanochrysum (black-gold philodendron) is exquisitely delicate and comes from Colombia and Costa Rica. At first the leaves are heart-shaped and have prominent veining; by the time the plant's leaves reach maturity they are velvety and elongated.

P. selloum (lacy tree philodendron). Its leaves can be up to 60cm/2ft long

P. panduraeforme (fiddle-leaf) can be trained to grow up a pole

P. 'Emerald Queen' is an F1 hybrid

PROBLEMS

If the leaves at the base of the plant turn yellow and fall, the plant is probably being overwatered. Reduce watering and allow soil to dry out between applications.

If the philodendron does not develop, ensure the plant is given the right conditions in both summer and winter. These plants need a contrast between seasons.

Brown tips may develop on the leathery leaves. Make sure the plant is out of strong direct sunlight.

Peperomia caperata

EASY

There are several hundred members of this small, bushy, herbaceous family which is characterized by a great variety of attractive and unusual leaves and colours.

Originally from tropical areas of Brazil, where it is found under the tree canopy, *Peperomia* grows to 10–15cm/4–6in high and often produces creamy white flower spikes. It also looks good in a hanging basket.

It likes warm, humid conditions, as in its native habitat, with bright but indirect sunlight. Spray the foliage daily and stand the pot over damp gravel to ensure adequate humidity.

This plant is past its best after 2–3 years when it becomes quite straggly. It can then be propagated.

PROBLEMS

Overwatering will cause leaf and stem rot, particularly in winter. Allow the compost almost to dry out between waterings.

Dry air will cause the leaves to turn brown and fall. Improve humidity by standing the pot over damp gravel and misting frequently.

Red spider mite will cause the leaves to go yellow with cobwebbing on the underside. Spray with systemic insecticide.

CARE

Light and temperature
Bright to semi-shady conditions with a temperature of around 21°C/70°F. It will tolerate temperatures as low as 10°C/50°F in winter if the compost is kept fairly dry.

Water and feeding
Keep moist all year round, but do not allow the compost to get soggy, especially in winter, or the roots and stem will rot. Ensure good humidity all year. Feed at monthly intervals in summer with a liquid solution.

Propagation
In spring or summer with leaf bud or stem cuttings into a good houseplant mixture.

Repotting
Only when potbound, in a soil-based compost.

Peperomia caperata 'Emerald Ripple' one of the small-leaved species

Raphis (Lady palm)

EASY

One of the most popular palms in America, there are many varieties of *Raphis*, which has delicate heads of fan-shaped leaves topping thin stems of unbranching 'bamboo'. Like many of the palms, *Raphis* comes from Southern China, where it grows in the tropical and shady rainforests, receiving little or no sunlight. It was introduced into Europe in the 1890s.

There are dwarf varieties available, growing to 60cm/2ft, and also varieties with variegated leaves that can occasionally be found for sale as indoor plants. The most commonly available are *Raphis excelsa*, which reaches 2m/80cm, and the somewhat smaller, more delicate, *Raphis humilis*.

The lady palm likes good air circulation and can look very decorative in a stairwell during the winter months, appreciating a spell on a warm patio outside in summer, providing it receives little sun. It makes an excellent conservatory plant.

Raphis excelsa can be bought in dwarf forms which have variegated leaves

CARE

Light and temperature
A semi-sunny location and good light. It will cope with cooler temperatures, 10°C/50°F in winter and average temperatures in summer. Avoid temperature fluctuations and draughts.

Water and feeding
Keep the compost evenly moist, watering freely in summer and less so in winter. It needs good humidity and the palmate fronds should be misted regularly. In summer feed every 7 days with a weak solution of liquid fertilizer.

Propagation
Shoots can be carefully separated from the main plant and potted up into loam-based compost. Nursery men propagate from seed at high temperatures, but as a houseplant *Raphis* will not flower or produce seed.

Repotting
Necessary only when the plant outgrows its pot. Use well-draining loam-based soil and move to a pot one size larger in spring.

PROBLEMS

Red spider mite can attack this plant. Spray with a systemic insecticide.

If the leaf tips of the fronds become brown, move the plant to a slightly cooler position and increase the humidity. Stand on a tray of pebbles.

Rhoeo discolor (Moses in the basket)

QUITE DIFFICULT

This striking plant has a short stem from which radiate a number of firm pointed dark green leaves that are purple underneath. It may produce spikes of white flowers.

Originally from the Central Americas, where its native habitat is along the Pacific coastline from Mexico into Central America, *Rhoeo* is quite a delicate houseplant. It likes a warm, humid position, away from draughts, and should be misted often with tepid soft water. The compost must never be allowed to get soggy, especially in winter.

Clean the leaves occasionally with a damp cloth and do not use leaf shine.

It should last for 2–3 years.

CARE

Light and temperature
Indirect light and a warm, constant temperature, ideally 18°C/64°F, all year, and no lower than 15°C/60°F in winter.

Water and feeding
Water carefully and ensure the compost is never soggy, especially in winter. Provide good humidity and mist often. Feed once a week in spring and summer with a liquid solution.

Propagation
In spring from side shoots or stem cuttings. Allow cuttings to dry out for a couple of days, then pot in a mixture of peat and sand.

Repotting
Each spring in a no. 2 peat-based compost.

PROBLEMS

This plant needs good humidity but is sensitive to overwatering. If the air is too dry the leaves will curl and turn brown, and if overwatered it will suffer stem rot. Allow to dry out before watering again.

Rhoeo discolor is also known as *R. bermudensis*, and the variegated form has pale creamy vertical stripes on the upper side of the leaf

Rhoicissus rhomboidea (Grape ivy, Natal vine)

EASY

This very versatile climbing plant has pretty dark green and glossy leaves that are made up of three smaller leaflets. Its native habitat is Cape Province, South Africa, where it grows almost anywhere in light shade. It was introduced into Europe in the 1940s and has become one of the most popular indoor plants.

Rhoicissus rhomboidea is the most commonly available variety, but *R. r.* 'Ellen Danica' is more unusual because its leaflets have lobes. *R. capensis* (Cape or evergreen grape) has large brown-edged leaves with brown and velvety undersides. It will, in exceptional circumstances, produce red berries.

All varieties can grow into large plants, up to 3m/10ft tall, and they are tuberous-rooted. They develop new growth freely and climb by using tendrils. They normally have a life expectancy of up to 10 years, but are susceptible to sudden wilt.

R. capensis has leaves up to 20cm/8in across

Rhoicissus rhomboidea grows either as a pot plant or can be trained as a climber on a moss pole

CARE

Light and temperature
A north- or east-facing window is best, as these plants do not like direct sunlight. In winter, temperatures should not fall below 15°C/60°F. Normal room temperature is fine in summer but the plants will not thrive if the room becomes stuffy.

Water and feeding
Keep the compost moist in summer, taking care not to overwater or the plant's leaves will go limp and rot. In winter, water every fortnight. Feed every 2 weeks with liquid plant food in summer. Moisten the leaves in summer and stand the plant on a tray of moist pebbles if possible.

Repotting
Once a year in spring, using fresh compost, until the plant reaches maturity. Then change the 5cm/2in of topsoil each year.

Propagation
Take stem-tip cuttings with 2 leaves, and root them in a mixture of half compost and half sand at a temperature of 18°C/64°. Repot into potting compost when cuttings have taken, in 21–28 days.

PROBLEMS

If signs of mildew fungus disease become obvious, reduce watering immediately and water less frequently.

Red spider mite or greenfly may attack this plant. Treat with a systemic insecticide.

Brown patches may develop on the leaves which will eventually drop off. Remove affected leaves. Improve the humidity if the atmosphere is dry.

If the leaves look drab, consider if the temperature is high enough. Overwatering may also be a cause.

Saxifraga stolonifera (Strawberry geranium)

QUITE EASY

This quite hardy plant comes from the temperate zones of China and Japan.

It is a small, dense plant with attractive round or kidney-shaped olive-green veined leaves which are pale purple underneath. It forms a number of runners with tiny plantlets on the end which trail over the edge of the pot, so it is best grown in a hanging basket. Small white star-shaped flowers are produced in summer. There is also a variegated version, 'Tricolor', with red, green and cream leaves which, being a little more fragile, requires a higher temperature.

S. stolonifera likes cool, bright conditions. A relatively quick grower when young it is best to propagate every 2–3 years as the plant can become straggly.

CARE

Light and temperature
Bright conditions, but not direct sunlight. The temperature should be quite cool all year round, and can go as low as 7°C/45°F in winter.

Water and feeding
Water 2–3 times a week in spring and summer and less in winter. In summer, feed every 2 weeks with a liquid solution and spray every 3 weeks to clean the leaves.

Propagation
It will produce small offshoots which often have roots. Plant several together in a mixture of soil, peat and sand and trim the stems.

Repotting
Each year in spring in a mixture of soil, peat and sand.

PROBLEMS

Take care not to overwater as this will cause stem rot. Allow to dry out and then water a little less.

If conditions are too warm, greenfly or aphids will be a problem. Spray with a systemic insecticide and move to a cooler position.

'Tricolor'

Saxifraga stolonifera bears its flowers in clusters on tall thin stalks

Schefflera (Umbrella tree, parasol plant)

EASY

The umbrella tree, so called as its leaves look like the spokes of an umbrella, is a sturdy and impressive houseplant with glossy palmate clusters of long-stemmed green leaves, sometimes variegated.

It is a quick grower, to a height of up to 3m/10ft, and benefits from frequent pruning to encourage a bushier plant.

Originally from the subtropical areas of Asia and Australia, *Schefflera actinophylla* grows into a substantial tree in its native habitat. Indoors it adapts to a range of temperatures all year round, and benefits from a spell outside in summer in a protected spot.

S. arboricola (Hawaiian elf) has an erect habit and clusters of blackish berries; it is a popular house plant.

Clean the leaves regularly with a damp cloth.

As a houseplant it is almost indestructible, and with good conditions should be everlasting.

CARE

Light and temperature
Bright or lightly shaded conditions with temperatures of 10–18°C/50–64°F throughout the year. It will withstand up to 27°C/80°F in summer.

Water and feeding
Water regularly in spring and summer, keeping the compost moist at all times. In temperatures above 18°C/64°F spray regularly. Feed with a liquid fertilizer at fortnightly intervals during summer. In winter water thoroughly but allow to dry out between waterings.

Propagation
By seed in spring or by root cuttings, both of which need to be established in a propagator at 21–24°C/70–75°F. This is quite difficult and best left to a professional.

Repotting
Pot on every year or two, as the plant becomes rootbound, in a rich soil- or peat-based compost.

PROBLEMS

Virtually problem free.

The foliage will turn brown if the plant is underwatered.

S. arboricola comes in several variegated forms, here *S.a. capello*

S. arboricola 'Trinette' has dainty leaves

S. 'Nora' is sometimes known as the octopus plant

Selaginella apoda (Basket selaginella, creeping moss)

QUITE EASY

This member of the *Selaginella* family has pale green moss-like leaves which form a dense mat of foliage. A favourite in Victorian times, it is only now enjoying a revival in popularity.

Originally from the warm temperate zones of the East Coast of North America, it does well in a terrarium as it dislikes dry air and draughty rooms.

Selaginella apoda should be grown in a shallow pot, away from direct light. The pot should be surrounded by damp peat and misted often. Use fresh tepid water for watering and misting and do not use leaf shine. It can grow quite quickly and can easily be cut back, by half if necessary.

It should last for 2 or 3 years.

Selaginella apoda can look effective in a mixed planting

CARE

Light and temperature
A shady to semi-shady position with warm constant temperatures, ideally 18–24°C/64–75°F all year.

Water and feeding
Water freely throughout the year and mist daily to ensure adequate humidity. Keep the soil moist but not soggy, and never let the compost dry out. Feed every 3 weeks in spring and summer with a liquid fertilizer.

Propagation
In spring, with cuttings planted in a growing mixture for 3–4 weeks. Once established move to its adult pot.

Repotting
In spring, in the same container, using a no. 2 peat-based compost with added leafmould.

PROBLEMS

Ensure adequate humidity otherwise the plant will not last.

Prone to aphids and spider mites. Treat aphids with a pyrethrum-based insecticide and mites with a systemic insecticide.

S. rubra is the red-leafed species

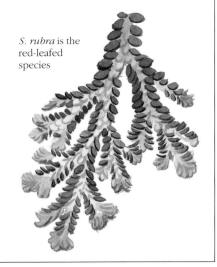

Senecio rowleyanus (String of pearls)

QUITE EASY

This trailing plant with succulent pea-like leaves hails from Southern Namibia where it can be found growing from the rocky outcrops in full sun. The plant will form dense mats.

It is best used in a hanging basket, either indoors or in a good sunny situation in a conservatory. There the beadlike leaves, which are marbled in greens and whites, can be seen to good advantage.

The common name of the plant is obvious once it is seen.

Good air circulation is important as these plants have been adapted from a naturally airy growing site.

CARE

Light and temperature
In summer in a sunny position. It will withstand a temperature up to 30°C/85°F. In winter keep in good light but the temperature may go down to 10°C/50°F.

Water and feeding
Allow the surface of the compost to dry out between waterings. Feed at monthly intervals during spring and summer with a general houseplant fertilizer at half strength.

Propagation
Break off 10cm/4in pieces of stem, allow to dry for 48 hours and pot into cactus compost at a temperature of 21°C/71°F.

Repotting
Every second year in a cactus compost.

PROBLEMS

Aphids may attack this plant. Spray with a systemic insecticide.

Senecio rowleyanus

Soleirolia soleirolii (Baby's tears, mind your own business)

QUITE EASY

This tiny-leaved ground-cover plant grows freely throughout the Mediterranean area in moist spots between paving stones or cracks in rocks. Despite its delicate appearance, it is a tenacious grower and can easily take over if not watched carefully. In the last few years it has become extremely popular.

As a houseplant it is particularly useful for hanging baskets or among a mixed arrangement.

It is a good idea to propagate new plants as the older ones pass their best. This is very easy to do.

CARE

Light and temperature
Bright, indirect light or semi-shady conditions with cool temperatures never above 21°C/70°F.

Water and feeding
Always keep the compost moist and never let it dry out, even in winter. Spray frequently if the temperature exceeds 21°C/70°F, otherwise at weekly intervals during spring and summer. Feed monthly in spring and summer with a liquid fertilizer.

Propagation
Any time of the year by dividing the plant into small sections which can be put into a good houseplant mixture – they will establish very quickly.

Repotting
In spring in a soil- or peat-based compost.

PROBLEMS

Virtually problem free.

The foliage will turn brown if the plant is underwatered.

Soleirolia soleirolii 'Helxine'

Tradescantia (Wandering Jew, inch plant)

EASY

Originally from Central America, Argentina and Brazil, this energetic creeper has smallish, shiny, oval green leaves with creamy yellow stripes and banks. In its native habitat it is found as a ground-cover and trailing plant. Its fast-growing stems, with their profusion of leaves, make it ideal for a hanging basket. New growth can be pinched out to encourage a denser plant.

Tradescantia is a good plant for the beginner as it accommodates a reasonable range of conditions and will not die if it misses out on the occasional watering. Its only disadvantage is that it tends to become straggly after a year or two and should be replaced by propagation, which is very easy.

It only needs to be misted occasionally, which should keep the leaves sufficiently clean.

From the same group as *Tradescantia* is the species *Zebrina*, which comes from Mexico. Strong direct light intensifies its leaf colours.

CARE

Light and temperature
Bright but indirect light, especially for variegated varieties, which need light to maintain their leaf colour. The ideal temperature is 18°C/64°F all year.

Water and feeding
Water 2–3 times a week in spring and summer and once a week in winter, allowing the soil almost to dry out between waterings. Mist occasionally. Fertilize every 2 weeks in spring and summer with a general houseplant solution.

Propagation
It is best to propagate each year in spring. Stem-tip cuttings will root easily in a mixture of loam and sand or in water, and have no special temperature requirements.

Repotting
Propagation is recommended.

PROBLEMS

If the leaves turn brown, the plant is either too dry or in too much light. Water more frequently and make sure it does not have direct sunlight.

Straggly growth means that the plant needs lighter conditions or that it is past its best and should be replaced by propagation.

Red spider mite and greenfly tend to attack this plant. Spray spider mite with a systemic insecticide and greenfly with a pyrethrum-based insecticide.

Zebrina pendula (silvery wandering Jew)

T. flumensis (Rio tradescantia) has small white flowers

T. albiflora tricolor (giant white inch plant) has large fleshy leaves

Zebrina pendula quadricolor (happy wandering Jew)

T. albiflora 'Albo-vittata'

Opposite: *Tradescantia*

Yucca elephantipes (Spineless yucca, pine lily)

EASY

This most exotic member of the lily family comes from the subtropical areas of Mexico and Guatemala, where it grows to a height of 15m/45ft in sunny, arid conditions.

The sturdy trunk is swollen at the base and from the top grow numerous rosettes of firm, glossy green, pointed leaves. It can also produce clusters of creamy white flowers.

Canes of 30cm–2m/1–6ft are now imported from the West Indies and Central America and quite often different stem lengths are potted together.

As a houseplant *Yucca elephantipes* is hardy and not at all temperamental, preferring a dry, sunny position, but also able to adapt to semi-shade. Mist occasionally. Wipe the leaves with a damp cloth from time to time but do not use leaf shine. The plant will benefit from a spell outdoors in summer.

It should live for many years.

Yucca elephantipes flowers after a number of years

CARE

Light and temperature
Bright light, even direct sunlight, especially in winter, though it will also be happy in a semi-shady position. It likes a temperature of 18–22°C/64–71°F all year, and no lower than 7°C/45°F in winter.

Water and feeding
Water thoroughly, but allow the compost almost to dry out between waterings. It will need less water in winter. Spray occasionally. Feed at fortnightly intervals in spring and summer.

Propagation
Side shoots will appear in spring that can be planted on individually in small pots in a mixture of no. 2 compost and sand. Maintain a constant temperature of 24°C/75°F until established.

Repotting
For young plants, repot every second year in a no. 2 compost mixed with sand. For mature plants it is necessary only to change the topsoil.

PROBLEMS

If the leaves turn yellow, the plant probably needs more light. Cut off the damaged leaves and move to a sunnier position.

Scale insect can attack this plant. Spray with a systemic insecticide.

Bromeliads

The glorious leaf colours of bromeliads are unforgettable and dramatic; they are showy plants and well worth having for the sharp colours of their flowers alone. Imagine a South American jungle filled with orchids and bromeliads, in all their brilliant colours, on the floor of the forest and attached to the trunks of trees.

There are over 1400 known species of bromeliad; in this book we have covered some of those most adaptable to cultivation as indoor plants. They should be watered through the natural well in the centre of the plant for, in their native habitat, the rain falls on the leaves and runs down into this well.

The mother plant of the bromeliad dies after flowering, leaving behind it 2 or 3 plantlets to grow on and replace it. Plants should ideally be purchased when the flower spathe is just beginning to emerge from the well.

Aechmea fasciata (Urn plant, Greek vase plant, bottle brush plant)

EASY

This plant, also known as *Billbergia rhodocynea*, comes from Brazil, where it was discovered in 1826. Naturally epiphytic, its natural habitat is on the floor of the jungle.

The name *Aechmea* derives from the Greek for lance tip – a reference to the sharply pointed central pink bract that is surrounded by long strap-shaped leaves. The actual flowers are small and blue, blooming on the edges of the spike in summer and lasting for up to 6 weeks. The plant forms a natural well that holds water in its centre.

After the flowers die, the pink spike slowly shrivels and at the same time replaces itself with 2 or 3 baby spikes or rosettes. Eventually these baby spikes can be repotted as individual plants, but the main plant will not bloom again for another year.

Aechmea will grow to 60cm/2ft across with leaves up to 30cm/1ft long. It will be 3 or 4 years old before the pink bract spikes appear and the plant flowers for the first time. There is a very striking variety called 'Purpurea' that has maroon-coloured leaves with silver markings.

Aechmea fasciata

CARE

Light and temperature
Aechmea is a very tolerant plant and can take either direct or indirect sunlight. The temperature should be no lower than 12°C/55°F and no higher than 27°C/80°F.

Water and feeding
Water twice a week and keep 2.5cm/½in water in the central spike. If possible, use rain water. Do not feed. Misting the leaves with weak solutions of fertilizer helps.

Propagation
The amateur finds offsets easier than raising seed. In springtime remove the offsets at the base of the plant once they look to be viable (after 4–6 months). Pot them on into a rich, barely moist potting compost. Do not separate the new rosette until the parent has completely shrivelled up.

Repotting
This is rarely required, but if needs be should be done at the onset of the growing period.

PROBLEMS

The flower stem may rot through overwatering at too low temperatures. Empty the rosette and allow the compost to dry out.

If the leaves develop brown tips and shrivel before flowering, the plant is getting too hot and dry. Increase watering.

If greenfly infests the plant, spray with diluted malathion.

Aechmea is also prone to scale insect and mealy bug, which should be treated with methylated spirit.

If bract spikes and flowers fail to appear move the plant to a sunnier situation.

Nidularium (Bird's nest)

EASY

This bromeliad, from tropical South America, is rarely seen. Like the *Neoregelia*, it has a central rosette of very short leaves. This 'bird's nest' turns bright red in summer during flowering time – the plant's name derives from the Latin word *nidus*, meaning nest. The stiff strappy leaves can grow to about 30cm/12in long. The white flowers are uninteresting and short-lived.

There are many varieties of this plant. *N. innocentii* has saw-edged leaves which are coloured purple above and wine-red underneath. *N innocentii striatum* has variegated leaves while *N. fulgens* (blushing cap) has spotted ones.

Nidularium innocentii

CARE

Light and temperature
Bright light, but away from direct midday sun. Again keep temperatures at about 15°C/60°F all year round.

Water and feeding
Ensure the central funnel is full of water at all times. During the summer months, keep the compost moist by watering once or twice a week. It requires high humidity so place it on a tray of wet pebbles.

Propagation
By offsets, which appear at the base of the plant. Wait until the mother plant has shrivelled completely after flowering, then separate the rosettes and pot them on into a sandy, well-draining compost. Keep them moist, at temperatures of 15°C/60°F.

Repotting
Only when separating plantlets or when seriously pot bound.

PROBLEMS

Overwatering will cause the plant to rot and die. Water the compost less often.

If the leaves develop brown tips, either the air is too dry or the plant is receiving insufficient water. Increase watering, using rain water if possible, and mist during summer.

Tillandsia lindenii (Blue-flowered torch)

EASY

This dramatic bromeliad has grass-like leaves and an eye-catching central pink bract with a flower head up to 30cm/12in long. The bracts bear deep blue flowers with white throats 5cm/2in across.

Like all bromeliads, its native habitat is in the tropical and subtropical areas of South America and it is an epiphyte, growing on rocks or on the trunks and in hollows of other trees and plants, which give it support. The plant can also thrive in arid desert.

Tillandsia cyanea (pink quill) has similar leaves but a more compact and smaller flower head, which is again coloured pink with plain blue flowers.

Both *Tillandsia cyanea* and *Tillandsia lindenii* are green-leaved bromeliads.

The tillandsias sold as pot plants are often either attached to a stone or growing from the branch of a tree. They have practically no roots, and feed and nourish themselves through their leaves. *Tillandsia usneoides* (air plant or Spanish moss) is the most commonly purchased of the grey tillandsias.

CARE

Light and temperature
Bright filtered light suits *Tillandsia*, but keep it away from direct midday sun. Average room temperatures should be maintained throughout the year.

Water and feeding
Keep the central funnel full of water at all times. As well, during the summer, keep the compost moist by watering once or twice a week. The plant should be stood on a tray of damp pebbles to increase humidity. Mist the leaves frequently. Do not feed.

Propagation
By offshoots which appear at the base of the plant as the spike starts to die back. Wait until the mother plant has completely shrivelled up after flowering before separating and potting on the new plantlets. Use a bromeliad soil or sandy compost. Keep moist, at a temperature of 15°C/60°F.

Repotting
Only when absolutely necessary.

PROBLEMS

If the flowers fail to appear in spring, move the plant to a lighter position.

Insufficient water or dry atmospheres can cause the leaf tips to brown. Increase watering, using rain water if possible, and mist the leaves often.

Rot can be caused by overwatering.

Opposite: *Tillandsia cyanea*

Vriesea splendens (Flame sword)

DIFFICULT

There are around 100 known species of *Vriesea*, one of the showiest of the bromeliads. It is named after the Dutch botanist, W. H. de Vriese and is a native of tropical Guyana.

V. splendens 'Major' is the most readily available variety. It has stiff strappy dark green leaves, with purple- or chocolate-coloured bands running across them, which grow up to 45cm/18in long.

The central bright orange bract gives the plant its common name of flaming sword. It may appear at anytime throughout the year and can last for months. In summer small yellow flowers develop, but only after the plant has been potted up for several years.

CARE

Light and temperature
3–4 hours a day of direct sunlight will force the bromeliad into flower. Hot midday sun should be avoided. Keep the temperature at around 15°C/60°F throughout the year.

Water and feeding
As for all bromeliads, liquid fertilizer should not be given. Keep the potting compost moist by watering once or twice a week in summer months and less frequently during the cooler times. Mist the leaves and stand the plant on a tray of moist pebbles to increase humidity.

Propagation
Offsets are formed in spring and can be separated from the parent plant after the plant spike has shrivelled completely. They should be cut away with a sharp knife and potted on into a well-drained sandy compost. Keep the temperature on the warm side and avoid draughts.

Repotting
Only when absolutely essential, if the plant is potbound.

PROBLEMS

Overwatering can cause the plant to rot. It will be difficult to rescue, but try cutting down on watering immediately.

If the bract spikes do not appear, move the plant to a sunnier situation in early spring.

If the atmosphere is too dry brown tips may develop at the end of the leaves. Increase humidity by placing the plant on a tray of moist pebbles.

The spathe of *Vriesea splendens* 'Major' should be removed after the flowers die

Ferns

Among the oldest plants known, there are some 250 species of fern found all over the world. They were fashionable in Victorian times and today their delicate and attractive leaves make them popular as indoor plants, particularly in mixed groupings.

Ferns reproduce themselves through spores and do not flower. Many of them grow naturally in deep shade in tropical forests; others are epiphytic, found attached high up on tree trunks or colonizing cliff tops in full sunshine. They are mostly rhizomes.

As indoor plants, all ferns will do well if given high humidity. Standing the plant on a tray of damp pebbles is essential for success, but plants do not like spray-misting on their leaves.

Adiantum (Maidenhair fern)

Adiantum fragrans

QUITE EASY

This most delicate of ferns, with dainty, fan-like, pale green triangular leaves on black wiry stalks, comes from the tropical and subtropical areas of Australia, New Zealand and the Americas, where it is to be found growing amongst rocks. Some hardy or nearly hardy varieties grow in the United Kingdom.

It is not difficult to grow indoors, but requires constant monitoring to ensure it does not dry out. This plant needs a steady, humid atmosphere with no direct sunlight, and does well in bathrooms and the shaded parts of a conservatory or greenhouse. Keep the roots moist, but not wet, and spray often, daily if in a heated room.

Adiantum will grow to 60cm/24in across and 30–38cm/12–15in high. There are some 200 varieties, but the most common ones available are *monocolor, fragrans, scuteum roseum* and 'Fritz Lutzii'.

It is a very long-lasting plant.

A. scuteum roseum   'Fritz Lutzii'   *A. monocolor*

CARE

Light and temperature
Adiantum grows well in warm, humid and sheltered spots away from direct sunlight. It dislikes both draughts and dry air. The minimum winter temperature is 10°C/50°F and the maximum summer temperature 24°C/75°F.

Water and feeding
The roots must not be allowed to dry out. It is best to submerge the pot in water for 10 minutes, then drain, probably twice weekly in summer and once a week in winter. Feed fortnightly with liquid fertilizer from mid-spring to mid-autumn or use slow-release pellets. These plants love a high degree of humidity in warm temperatures. Spray leaves daily and stand the container on moist pebbles.

Propagation
In spring divide the clumps, leaving a piece of rhizome attached to each clump, and place in a good peat-based compost to which you have added a little fertilizer.

Repotting
Repot in a peat-based compost each spring. Pack the soil lightly as good drainage is essential.

PROBLEMS

Most problems arise from a lack of moisture and humidity.

If the fronds dry up, cut them off and spray daily until new shoots appear.

If the leaves drop, the plant can be cut right back to encourage new growth. Continue watering and spraying while it becomes established.

If the leaves turn pale, the plant has received too much sunlight. Move it out of the sun and into a shadier position.

Asplenium nidus (Bird's nest fern)

EASY

This exotic forest fern comes from the humid tropical areas of South East Asia and Australia, where it grows as an epiphyte in protected but constantly damp positions.

It forms a handsome rosette of lance-shaped, bright green leaves with dark central veins which will grow to almost 1m/3ft in length. These leaves are very delicate and should be cleaned carefully with a damp cloth from time to time. Do not use leaf shine.

Asplenium does well as a houseplant. It is a relatively quick grower and is at its best for 3 years, after which it should be propagated (which is difficult to do at home).

It likes a warm, humid and partly shady spot, away from draughts, but can tolerate central heating if there is sufficient humidity.

A. nidus

Asplenium nidus

CARE

Light and temperature
A semi-shady position, away from direct sunlight. The ideal temperature is 20°C/68°F all year, and no lower than 16°C/61°F in winter.

Water and feeding
Water 2–3 times a week in summer to keep the compost moist at all times. In winter water less, allowing the top of the compost almost to dry out between waterings. To ensure adequate humidity, stand the pot over damp pebbles. In spring and summer fertilize with a general houseplant solution at fortnightly intervals.

Propagation
By spore. This is difficult and best left to a professional.

Repotting
This plant does not like to be moved unnecessarily so pot on in summer only when it has become rootbound.

PROBLEMS

Prone to scale insect, which should be treated with a systemic insecticide.

Damaged or dried fronds can be cut off at the stem.

Brown spots on the leaves mean that the position is too cold and draughty. Move to a warmer, more protected spot.

Nephrolepis (Sword fern, Boston fern, fishbone fern)

EASY

This common fern, with long tapering fronds that can grow up to 1m/3ft, was a favourite in Victorian times.

It grows freely in all tropical regions of the world, from Africa to the Americas and the Far East. A good humidity is essential, and it likes warm, bright, but semi-shady conditions (as it enjoys in its native habitat) all year round.

Spray each day with tepid rain water and stand the pot over wet gravel. Never allow the compost to dry out or to become water-logged.

It is a good houseplant as it will tolerate a fairly dark position, but it does not always do well in a centrally heated room or close to a gas fire. In the right conditions *Nephrolepis* will last a long time.

Do not use insecticides or leaf shine on this plant.

PROBLEMS

Sometimes the fern will deteriorate for no apparent reason. Cut it down to just above soil level and keep warm and humid until it begins to grow again.

Dry and dropping leaves are caused by dry air. Immerse the pot in water, drain, surround the pot with damp peat, and spray daily. If it does not recover, cut it right back and treat as above.

Scale insect and mealy bug can be attracted to this plant. Remove with a cloth dipped in methylated spirit. Do not use an insecticide.

CARE

Light and temperature
Bright to semi-shady conditions, but no direct sunlight and no dry air. In summer temperatures should be 18–24°C/64–75°F and in winter 13–16°C/55–61°F.

Water and feeding
Water 2–3 times a week with room temperature water in spring and summer, and feed each week with a weak liquid fertilizer. For the rest of the year water a little less, but never allow the compost to dry out.

Propagation
From plantlets that form on runners coming out of the crown of the plant. Pot these in a peaty mixture and keep at a constant temperature of 20°C/68°F until established.

Repotting
Repot in a peat-based mixture in spring as it becomes rootbound. The plant can be divided into smaller sections at the same time.

N. cordata

'Teddy Junior'

Nephrolepis exaltata bostoniensis (the Boston fern) was, surprisingly enough, discovered in that city in 1894 and will tolerate air-conditioning

Pellaea rotundifolia (Button fern, cliff brake)

QUITE EASY

Although a fern, this native of the temperate forests of New Zealand produces a profusion of thin black stems from which grow small, arched fronds of dark green leathery leaflets. The fronds reach 20cm/8in in length and will trail over the pot, making the plant ideal for a hanging basket.

Unusually, *Pellaea* prefers fairly dry conditions. The compost must never be allowed to become waterlogged or the plant will die. It does not appreciate misting either.

If conditions are right the plant will not have a rest period and should continue to grow all year round.

CARE

Light and temperature
Fairly bright but indirect light with constant temperatures, preferably not above 21°C/71°F. Increase humidity as the temperature rises. In winter it will tolerate as low as 6°C/43°F.

Water and feeding
Keep the compost moist, but never soggy, taking care not to let the plant dry out completely. Feed with a liquid solution of general houseplant fertilizer once a week during summer.

Propagation
Divide the rhizome into 2 or 3 sections, each with roots and some growth, and establish in a mixture of loam, peat and sand.

Repotting
Pot on as needed in a shallow pot, ensuring good drainage.

PROBLEMS

Never allow the compost to get soggy or the plant will die.

Susceptible to scale insect, mealy bug and aphids. Remove scale insect and mealy bug with a cloth dipped in methylated spirit. Spray aphids with a pyrethrum-based insecticide.

Pellaea rotundifolia bears little resemblance to the commonly perceived fern

Flowering Plants

Nursery men the world over are constantly seeking to improve the quality of our flowering plants: producing bigger blooms, lasting for longer periods, with new colours and greater readiness to flower.

None the less we have a wealth of beautiful and fragrant flowering plants to choose from throughout every season of the year. There are plants with richly fragrant flowers such as *Gardenia* and *Stephanotis*. There are those that are easy to grow like *Chrysanthemum* or *Clivia*, which has dramatic orange flower heads. And there are the challenging plants, such as *Columnea* or *Medinilla* – growing these successfully can be enormously rewarding.

The overriding factor for that success is the correct amount of light. After all, the flowering plants we propagate and you purchase have been adapted from ones that grow in the wild in the subtropical and tropical regions of the world. In this book, I have described these conditions so that cultivation at home can emulate them as closely as possible.

Achimenes (Hot water plant, nut orchid)

QUITE EASY

Achimenes, a member of the gesneriad family, has been popular for some 100 years

There are many folk myths associated with *Achimenes*, a plant early settlers in the United States took on their travels. Originally from Guatemala, it grows in high humidity in semi-shaded conditions.

A weak-stemmed plant, it bears masses of white, pink, blue, purple or yellow flowers throughout summer. Because its stems are weak, it is ideal for a hanging basket, where the flowers can trail downwards. It has hairy heart-shaped, jagged-edged leaves and grows up to 30cm/1ft high. After 2 or 3 years discard the plant.

There are several varieties. *Achimenes erecta* is a trailer, bearing bright red flowers. *Achimenes longiflora* has purple flowers, and there is a white variety as well. The tallest species is *Achimenes grandiflora*, which can grow to 60cm/2ft, but this is hard to find. More easily available are the *Achimenes* hybrids, which include 'Master Ingram', 'Rose Little Beauty' and 'Pink Beauty' (or 'Charm'), 'Purple King' and 'Paul Arnold'. These hybrids have been popular since the 1840s. Their flowering season is from early summer through to autumn. Never place *Achimenes* in direct sun.

CARE

Light and temperature
Bright light away from direct summer sun. Warm humid conditions with an average temperature of 13°C/55°F throughout the growing season.

Water and feeding
Never let this plant dry out, even for a single day. Spray occasionally. Feed once a fortnight with a weak liquid fertilizer during the flowering season. After blooms have finished, allow the plant to rest. Stimulate growth the following spring by watering with tepid water or else remove the rhizomes from the soil in autumn, and allow to dry off throughout the winter.

Propagation
Divide the peculiarly scaly rhizomes in early spring and plant up to 6 together in a pot about 15cm/6in across, or take cuttings in late spring in seed-raising compost and place in a propagator at a temperature of 21°C/70°F.

Repotting
The rhizomes need repotting in early spring, with the top 2.5cm/1in of soil being replaced with rich humus compost. It is easy to divide rhizomes when repotting.

PROBLEMS

Cobwebs forming on the underside of leaves indicate red spider mite. Spray with a systemic insecticide and do not allow the plant to dry out.

Leaves may become discoloured – spray less often.

If flowers do not form increase humidity and place in a lighter position, but avoiding direct sunlight.

Aphelandra squarrosa (Zebra plant, saffron spike)

DIFFICULT

There are many species of this plant, but only 2 have been hybridized as houseplants. By far the most commonly found is *Aphelandra squarrosa*, known as the zebra plant because of its distinctive leaf markings. Originally from tropical South America, this plant is greedy when it comes to humidity. Try to site it in a spot where it can stand on a tray of pebbles.

In domestic circumstances *Aphelandra* will be difficult to keep going for more than a year – leaves will fall from the base upwards and it usually becomes leggy. The stems are almost black, in stark contrast to the handsome yellow bract which appears for a month or more in autumn.

Aphelandra squarrosa 'Dania' has a striking golden bract, from which stem insignificant white flowers (though breeding by nursery men has improved this variety), and *Aphelandra squarrosa* 'Louisae' has bracts with deep orange tops. Both form reasonably bushy plants of up to 45cm/½in high and wide.

CARE

Light and temperature
Aphelandra likes bright light but no direct sun. The leaves burn easily. In summer keep at 18–27°C/64–80°F. After flowering has taken place in autumn, temperatures can drop to 12°C/55°F. Cold air will cause it to drop its leaves, as will too much sun and any hint of draughts.

Water and feeding
Always use soft warm water and never let the compost dry out. – waterlogging is fatal. Spray the leaves each day with warm water and cut off all faded bracts above a good pair of leaves. From early spring to early autumn feed on a weekly basis, and twice a week when the plant is in flower.

Propagation
In early spring take stem cuttings from leaf axils, preferably with 2 pairs of leaves, and pot up using a rooting hormone. A heated propagator must be used, and once new leaves signal the cutting has taken, pot on into a 15cm/6in container. Acclimatize the young plant carefully.

Repotting
If you have a sufficiently good specimen, repot it in spring in good compost.

PROBLEMS

Major leaf loss and brown leaf tips can be caused by dryness at the roots, even for a very short time. Other possible causes are too much sun, draughts or cold air and lack of humidity.

Cobwebs may form on the underside of leaves, indicating red spider mites caused by dryness. Use a systemic insecticide.

White woolly patches in the axils of leaves are caused by mealy bug. Spray with diluted malathion.

Aphelandra squarrosa 'Dania' has most dramatic creamy veining on its leaves

Azalea indica (Indian azalea)

QUITE DIFFICULT

Azaleas bring a sunburst of colour into the house, from scarlet to apricot to white. A member of the *Rhododendron* family and originating from China and Thailand, they are dwarf shrubs that can grow up to 45cm/1.5ft in height.

Azalea indica, or the Indian azalea, is by far the most popular. It has rich green leaves of up to 4cm/1.5in long with hairy undersides and the flowers are open and bell-shaped. It is forced into flower for winter colour but will suffer thereafter, and should not be neglected if the plant is to last until the following season.

Azaleas are usually bought when in flower. Pick one with a mass of buds, rather than blooms, so you can enjoy the spectacular show of flowers, either single or double, on top of the little flat bush. It should be watered by the immersion method (see page 232) perhaps every day when in flower.

After flowering, keep watering and place it outside during the summer. This variety is not frost-hardy, so the plant must be brought into the house when summer is over.

Azalea indica

'Osta'   'Indica'   'Inga'

CARE

Light and temperature
A pot-grown azalea loves cool temperatures. It likes good light but not direct sunshine, so a north-facing window is ideal.

Water and feeding
Keep the compost wet but not soggy at all times, using rain water. Remember azaleas hate lime. An occasional spray with rain water helps to prolong the life of the blooms. Pick off faded flowers promptly.

If you feed the plant each fortnight it should flower again the next autumn. In spring, after the danger of frost has passed, take the pot outside and place it in a light but cool place. Keep the compost wet all season before bringing it indoors in autumn.

Propagation
Cuttings of healthy young shoots around 7cm/3in can be taken in summer and rooted in a heated propagator in the middle of summer at temperatures of 21–24°C/ 70–75°F. Use only lime-free compost and keep moist with rain water.

Repotting
After the first season and when the plant has outgrown the pot, repot in spring, always using lime-free compost and keep in the garden throughout summer.

PROBLEMS

Shrivelled or yellowing leaves, or a short flowering period are the most common complaints. Always water azaleas thoroughly, if possible soaking the entire pot each week at least. Water with soft water and always use lime-free compost.

Lime in the water causes yellowing leaves. This indicates chlorosis, caused by a lack of iron if grown in lime soil. Treat with multi-tonic and pick off the affected leaves.

Too much sun will cause the flowers to wither and brown and then drop off, as will too little humidity and too much hot dry air. Keep azaleas well away from radiators.

Beloperone guttata (Shrimp plant)

EASY

Beloperone guttata is sometimes listed as *Justicia brandegeana*

CARE

Light and temperature
The stems of the shrimp plant become quite woody and if there is too much heat they will become softened and the plant will grow straggly. Temperatures of 20°C/71°F in summer and 18°C/64°F in winter will suit this plant. To produce colourful bracts it will need direct sunlight. This should be for relatively short periods in summer on a windowsill.

Water and feeding
Keep moist but not wet from spring to autumn, but drier in the winter months. Feed each fortnight during summer with a weak solution of houseplant fertilizer.

Propagation
In spring cut back the stems to 10cm/3in above the soil and repot at the same time. Tips of shoots can be rooted in a propagator at 18°C/64°F.

Repotting
In spring, prune back plants to around half their size and repot in good compost.

PROBLEMS

The plant will lose leaves if it becomes rootbound. Repot if necessary.

If leaves turn yellow, the plant has been overwatered. Allow the compost to dry out thoroughly before watering again.

Spray the plant with insecticide if it is attacked by aphids during hot weather; this is all too common.

If bracts do not develop, prune especially hard at the onset of the dormant period, and in early spring place the plant on an extremely sunny windowsill.

This small oval-leafed plant can survive for many years and grows up to 90cm/3ft square. Keep pruning out the stem tips to make the plant bushier and disregard those who tell you it is an annual.

The reddy-orange flower bracts are like overlapping Tuscan roof tiles and support a white flower which emerges at the end. The bracts appear almost all year round but the white flowers are insignificant and short-lived.

Beloperone guttata's native habitat is the tropical areas of Mexico, where it grows under tall trees. As an indoor plant it is very adaptable and cuttings can be rooted easily. There is a yellow form called 'Yellow Queen', which may be found on supermarket shelves from time to time.

Clever use can be made of this plant in hanging baskets.

Begonia elatior

EASY

There are around 900 different species of *Begonia*, which is named after the Frenchman Michel Begon (1638–1710), who was a patron of botanical science.

Some species are grown for their leaf colour; others, including *Begonia elatior*, for their flowers. Two English nursery men – Veitch in the 1880s and Clibrans in the 1900s – developed *B. elatior*, which is a native of Brazil, and Dutch specialists began marketing it just after World War II.

The plant is covered by a mass of single or double flowers in cheerful colours. It can be bought in flower at any time of year and indoors will last for about 3 months.

The German *Begonia elatior* 'Reiger' strain is among the most reliable varieties, with a long-lasting flowering period, and *Begonia elatior* 'Reigers Schwabenland' is particularly recommended.

Pinching out the growing tips when the plant is young will keep it bushy. It is normally discarded after flowering, though it is possible to keep it going through 2 or 3 flowerings.

Begonia tuberosa

Begonia elatior 'Reiger'

Begonia elatior

The flower head of *Begonia elatior*

Begonia elatior in its varied colours

B. tuber-hybrida 'Harlequin'

CARE

Light and temperature
Begonia prefers a light position, but not direct sunlight, which will scorch the leaves and flowers. Temperatures above 20°C/70°F are best avoided.

Water and feeding
When the plant is in flower, water often, but do not allow the soil to become soggy. Spray the foliage and flowers to keep moist air around the plant, but do not do this when the plant is in direct sunlight. Feeding is not strictly necessary, as the plant is usually discarded after flowering.

Propagation
Some varieties, like the double orange 'Charisma', can be raised from seed. Otherwise, new shoots can be used as cuttings.

Repotting
If raising from seed, pot on the seedlings only once after they reach flowering size.

PROBLEMS

Begonia is prone to powdery mildew. Cut off the diseased leaves and spray with a systemic fungicide. Improving ventilation and cutting back on watering often helps.

Botrytis causes brown, grey and mouldy patches and can be avoided by the same treatments as for powdery mildew.

Aphids and red spider mites need to be sprayed with appropriate insecticides.

Too little light and too little or too much water can cause yellowing of the leaves. If stems become long and leggy, there is inadequate light. Leaves will curl up if there is too much heat and they will rot and droop if the plant is overwatered.

The leaves will need to be sprayed with water if they develop brown tips.

If the plant collapses, the causes are most often stem rot disease (caused by overwatering), swollen bumps on the tubers (known as root knot), eelworm or vine weevil, which causes tunnels in the tuberous stems.

Bougainvillea glabra (Paper flower)

DIFFICULT

This is a glorious tropical climber, with dazzling purplish-pink bracts in groups of three which develop in spring and summer and last a long time. It is not an easy houseplant to grow or to make bloom again the next season. The stems are woody with spines and the leaves are narrow and smooth. In its native habitat of Brazil, it will grow to 9m/30ft but reaches considerably less when kept in a pot.

There are many different species, but I would say the most successful is *Bougainvillea glabra* 'Alexandra'. *Bougainvillea spectabilis* is altogether larger with stout spines. Its bracts measure up to 5cm/2in square and the plant has a spreading habit. Commonly found varieties include the American 'Crimson Lake' or 'Scarlett O'Hara' and the European 'Amethyst' and 'White Dania'.

This plant needs to be pruned in autumn and kept cool throughout the winter. Many bougainvilleas are available trained on hoops but they can also be found as standards or bushes.

'White Dania'

'Amethyst'   'Afterglow'

Bougainvillea glabra 'Alexandra'

CARE

Light and temperature
Keep the plant warm in summer; it will appreciate a spell outdoors baking in the sun. Maintain a minimum winter temperature of 7°C/45°F.

Water and feeding
When spring arrives, increase watering from once a fortnight to 2–3 times a week and feed the plant every 2 weeks with a weak solution of liquid fertilizer. It will need doses of potassium fertilizer each spring. Spray with tepid water on warm days and keep the compost moist in spring and summer, but almost dry in winter.

Propagation
In spring. Use 8–10cm/3–4in cuttings dipped in hormone rooting powder. Place in a propagator at a constant temperature of 21–24°C/70–75°F with high humidity. Many of the leaves may drop. This is, however, a difficult plant to root and propagation is best left to professionals.

Repotting
Repot in spring, and only when the existing pot has been outgrown. Use standard compost to which has been added some woodash. Sphagnum peat moss also helps.

PROBLEMS

Bad ventilation and a humidity level that is too high will cause mealy bugs. Spray with an insecticide.

Cobwebs underneath the leaves are caused by red spider mite due to the plant becoming dry. Use a systemic insecticide.

Yellowing of leaves is caused by the plant being too wet. Always ensure the compost has very good drainage.

Bouvardia (Sweet bouvardia, scarlet trompetilla)

DIFFICULT

This is a gloriously scented plant with trusses of pink or white 4-lobed flowers which come out from summer through to midwinter. Originally from Mexico, it is similar to *Ixora* as both of these species belong to the madder family.

Bouvardia lasts for only a couple of years, even when it has had the most expert and loving attention. It is valued for the time of year it blooms and for its scent as much as anything else.

Prune it vigorously in early spring and keep it on the dry side through a good period of rest during the early summer months.

CARE

Light and temperature
Bright light, but keep shaded from direct summer sun. Minimum temperatures of 10°C/50°F in autumn help to set flower buds. Room temperature in summer.

Water and feeding
Water freely while the plant is flowering and feed each fortnight. After flowering, allow compost to dry out between waterings.

Propagation
Through stem cuttings taken in spring.

Repotting
Should be repotted each spring in a mixture of general purpose soil, perlite and peat.

B. longifolia has the most delightful scented white flowers

Bouvardia 'Bridesmaid'

B. ternifolia can bear its scarlet blossoms for much of the year

PROBLEMS

Webs on the underside of leaves indicate red spider mite. Spray with a systemic insecticide and raise humidity.

If the plant droops it is too cold or too dry.

If the leaves dry out move the plant to a cooler spot.

Browallia (Bush violet, amethyst flower, sapphire flower)

EASY

With proper care and attention, this dainty, simple plant can bloom for weeks. In fact it is often bought for its long flowering period and then thrown out. *Browallia speciosa* flowers naturally during the second half of the year, depending on the time of sowing, and looks particularly effective when massed with others as a group.

From tropical Colombia, the plant grows up to 50cm/20in in height and has dark green leaves with blue, lavender and white flowers. Some plants need stakes to support the stems. The more the plant is pinched out in its early growing days the better. You should pick off the dead flowers regularly and discard the plant when the flowering season is over.

The variety 'Major' produces large blue flowers, while 'Alba' has white blooms. The only other *Browallia* found as an indoor plant is *Browallia viscosa*, which is smaller than the bush violet and has white-throated flowers that are more subtle.

The bush violet, being a member of the deadly nightshade family, and therefore poisonous, should be kept well out of the reach of children and animals.

Browallia speciosa can look extremely effective in a hanging basket

CARE

Light and temperature
Browallia likes a bright position, but not direct sunlight. Give it 4 good hours of strong light a day. It needs to be in temperatures of around 20°C/68°F in summer (temperatures much over this will reduce the life of the flowers), and cooler in winter.

Water and feeding
In summer water often, always keeping the soil moist, and feed each week. In winter water sparingly, otherwise the roots may rot. Humidity is important so if possible place on a tray of wet pebbles.

Propagation
This plant grows easily from seed; sow in early spring. The seeds will sprout within 14 days. Cover with a dusting of compost and place in a propagator at 18°C/64°F. After the seedlings have germinated, prick off into 7.5cm/3in pots. They will begin to flower 6 months later.

Repotting
Not necessary as most people regard this plant as an annual.

PROBLEMS

When the air is dry, greenfly and whitefly can sometimes be a nuisance. Spray with insecticide.

If the plant becomes leggy, pinch out the growth tips to encourage bushiness.

Brunfelsia (Yesterday, today and tomorrow or morning, noon and night)

QUITE EASY

The common name of this sweet-smelling plant refers to its changing colours: the flowers move from purple through pale violet to white in fast succession.

It is an extremely slow growing but very attractive plant, with glossy green leaves and pretty flowers about 5cm/2in across. In its native habitat of Brazil, where it is found in tropical conditions under semi-shaded canopy, it will grow to 2m/8ft tall, but as an indoor plant it rarely reaches above 60cm/2ft. It can flower almost all year round, and will be particularly encouraged if placed in a sheltered spot on a sunny patio during the summer months.

CARE

Light and temperature
Keep out of direct sun when growing and in flower. During spring and summer keep temperature between 18–24°C/64–75°F. This plant flush flowers so to encourage a second flowering it is important to drop the temperature to 13°C/55°F. After this second flush and with winter approaching, reduce temperatures further to 7°C/45°F to harden off plant.

Water and feeding
Water thoroughly in spring and summer. Stand the pot on a saucer of pebbles almost covered with water since the plant enjoys high humidity. In winter, remove from pebbles and allow to dry out between waterings. During spring and summer feed at monthly intervals with general houseplant fertilizer.

Propagation
Take tip cuttings and place in cutting compost in a propagator at a temperature between 18–21°C/64–70°F.

Repotting
In autumn, when flowering has finished, in no. 2 loam-based compost.

PROBLEMS

Webs on underside of leaves indicate red spider mite. Use systemic insecticide or diluted malathion and raise humidity.

Grey mould may occur in winter if plant is too cold and too wet.

Brunfelsia pauciflora calycina can be found with white or yellow flowers as well as the more common purple variety

Campanula isophylla (Italian bellflower, star of Bethlehem, falling stars)

EASY

Nearly all campanulas are hardy garden plants, but only a few of the 35 genera are suitable as houseplants. By far the most reliable and dazzling of these is *Campanula isophylla*. With its pale green leaves setting off star-shaped blue or white flowers, it is best displayed from a suspended pot or hanging basket. Although blue is the most common colour, a white variety, *Campanula isophylla* 'alba', and a mauve variety, *Campanula isophylla* 'Mayii' (which is difficult to grow), are more readily available these days.

This pretty subtropical plant is a native of Italy and grows to a height of 22cm/9in with a spread of 45cm/18in. It should flower happily throughout the summer. Pinch off flower heads that have faded, and give the bush a sharp trim as the flowering season ends. The plant should be replaced after a couple of years.

C. isophylla 'alba'

C. isophylla

CARE

Light and temperature
Campanula likes bright positions with as much light as possible, but in summer protect it from the hot noon sun. It likes average warmth. Good periods of rest in winter will help the plant to be a successful flowerer the following season. In winter it will tolerate below-freezing temperatures. Adequate ventilation is essential.

Water and feeding
In the flowering season keep the plant moist at all times. Apply liquid fertilizer every fortnight to prolong the blooms. In late winter, cut the plant right back to within 3cm/1in of the soil, leaving 1 pair of leaves. Keep on the dry side, watering only occasionally. Vigorous new growth will appear in spring. Then water the plant regularly. Do not use leaf shine.

Propagation
Start cuttings off in spring from prunings made when cutting the plant back. Tips need to be 10cm/4in long and inserted into a peat and sand compost and placed in a propagating frame with a constant temperature of 18°C/64°F.

Repotting
Repot once in spring, after the first season, using a rich humus potting soil.

PROBLEMS

If leaves turn yellow and fall, red spider mites could be infesting the plant. Spray with a systemic insecticide.

Conditions that are too wet and cold cause flowers to rot and fall before opening. Stand in a warmer atmosphere and allow to dry out before watering again.

Waterlogging can cause the leaves and stems to rot. Allow the plant to dry out.

Should mould appear, apply a fungicide to kill the fungus. Make sure the compost is not left saturated in humid conditions.

C. carpatica 'Karl Foster'

C. carpatica 'Karl Foster' white

C. poscharskyana white

C. poscharskyana blue

Capsicum annuum (Ornamental chilli pepper, Christmas pepper)

EASY

CARE

Light and temperature
The plant needs to be in a sunny and airy position, but not too hot. Some direct sun is needed. In dim light, it will immediately shed its fruit. It prefers moderate temperatures.

Water and feeding
Keep damp, but not wet, and feed weekly during the growing period with weak solutions of liquid fertilizer.

Propagation
Ornamental chilli peppers can be grown from seed planted in a propagator in winter. If the seedlings are placed outside on a warm patio during summer they will bear more fruit than those continuously indoors.

Repotting
These plants are annuals.

Capsicum fruits profusely and the peppers last up to 3 months

Capsicum annuum is usually available in autumn, when its bright red fruits add festive cheer to windowsills and tables in the period leading up to Christmas.

The plant should be purchased in September, when the starlike white flowers are in bud. From these develop green peppers which ripen into purple, crimson and orangy-yellow edible fruits. It must not be confused with the poisonous *Solanum pseudocapsicum*. The plant grows to a height of 45cm/18in, and lasts only 1 season.

The ornamental pepper is native to Central South America, where it grows as a small tropical shrub.

PROBLEMS

Aphids and spider mites can infest the plant if it is put in a place which is too warm and dry. Move to a cooler position and spray with insecticide.

If the peppers fall the chances are the compost has been allowed to dry out. Increase watering. If this appears not to be the cause, increase humidity by placing the pot over a saucer of damp gravel.

Chrysanthemum

EASY

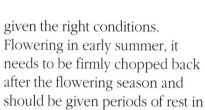

Potted chrysanthemums are now available all year round in almost every colour except blue. The Danes and the Dutch are developing many new and better varieties, with single or double flowers, in dwarf sizes, bushes or standards.

Chrysanthemum morifolium, or the florists' chrysanthemum, has been cultivated for over 3000 years in China and Japan, where it grows to 1m/3¼ft high and flowers naturally after the summer. The variety sold in stores today is *Chrysanthemum indicum*, which has been adapted to last longer in flower and is raised with the use of both chemicals and light restriction (the first curtailing growth; the second forcing flowering to a specific date). This plant is sold at a height of 24–30cm/9–12in and flowers throughout the year. It should be bought with coloured buds since green buds may fail to open.

Chrysanthemum frutescens (the white marguerite, or the Boston or Paris daisy) is altogether different and grows up to 90cm/36in high and 60cm/24in wide. It is also known as *Argyranthemum frutescens chrysaster*. The bush is covered by masses of small yellow or white daisy-shaped flowers which bloom for weeks on end. It may last for 3–4 years,

given the right conditions. Flowering in early summer, it needs to be firmly chopped back after the flowering season and should be given periods of rest in a greenhouse.

C. morifolium can be planted in the garden when flowering is over; this is a better long-term solution than trying to make these forced specimens last a second flowering period.

The flowering season lasts 6–8 weeks if sited in a bright, cool room; overheated rooms cause the plant to have a short life.

CARE

Light and temperature
Chrysanthemums need to be kept cool, around 13–16°C/55–60°F and in a bright position. Pot chrysanthemums must not be subjected to direct midday sun.

Water and feeding
In summer the plant needs to be kept thoroughly moist, which may mean watering it frequently. In winter, keep the compost just moist. Feed with fertilizer each fortnight while the plant is in flower.

Propagation
C. frutescens and *C. morifolium* can be raised from seed or cuttings in spring and potted into large containers of soil-based compost as necessary. They can then be brought indoors in the autumn, which is the natural flowering time for garden chrysanthemums. Pot-grown dwarf chrysanthemums can be pruned and planted outside in the garden after flowering, or be treated as annuals and discarded. If planted outdoors, they revert to the natural flowering season in autumn and grow taller as the effect of the dwarf hormones given to them by nursery men wears off.

Repotting
In spring, when necessary, using good potting compost.

PROBLEMS

Aphids and spider mites can infest the plants if they are too warm. Move to a cooler spot and spray with insecticide.

Chrysanthemum frutescens

Citrus mitis (Calamondin orange)

QUITE EASY

This miniature orange tree brings threefold pleasure. Its leaves are wonderfully glossy and dark green and carry deliciously fragrant tiny white flowers, borne singly on the branch tips, and decorative edible, if bitter, fruits.

From the Philippines, *Citrus mitis* is a dwarf variety and grows up to 1.2m/4ft high. It may well be a hybrid of the lime and the kumquat. Flowers and fruits develop throughout the year, though the greatest profusion will come in summer. A spell in the garden during this time will benefit the orange tree and may avoid the need to brush-pollinate the flowers. Midday is the best time to artifically aid pollination.

A gentle shake when buying the plant will ensure you do not choose one whose leaves are falling – a sign of an unhealthy specimen. Draughts should be avoided at all times. With good plant management *Citrus mitis* can last for years.

CARE

Light and temperature
Citrus mitis likes a bright, sunny position throughout the year and a spell outdoors in summer. In winter, temperatures of 15–18°C/60–64°F will suit it well. Good ventilation without draughts is important.

Water and feeding
Always use soft water and do not let the soil dry out between spring and autumn. In the growing period, use a weak solution of fertilizer each week.

Propagation
This is difficult to do in the domestic environment, but enthusiasts can try in spring. Dip cuttings in a rooting hormone powder and plant into a rich compost in a base-heated propagator. Plants grown from orange pips are too large for indoor plants in the long run.

Repotting
Lack of new growth indicates soil exhaustion. Repot in spring into a pot one size up when the plant is very potbound.

PROBLEMS

Citrus is prone to scale insect. Remove individually with methylated spirit swabs.

Spider mites, aphids and mealy bug may attack the plant from time to time. Spray with fungicides or insecticides.

If the leaves develop patches of dark grey mould, spray with a systemic fungicide.

Yellow leaves may appear if the plant has been watered using hard water. They may also be a sign of lack of magnesium. Add a plant tonic with magnesium to remedy this.

Brown-tipped leaves indicate the plant may be suffering from draughts. Move to a better site.

Citrus mitis has loose-skinned fruits around 5cm/2in across; they make a good addition to marmalade

Clerodendrum thomsonae

EASY   (Glory bower, bleeding heart vine)

This is a vigorous climbing shrub in the tropical regions of west Africa, where it grows up to 4m/13ft on twining stems, supporting itself on other vegetation. It has attractive dark glossy leaves with startling papery white flowers that have blood-red corollas appearing throughout the summer season.

Here nursery men treat the plant with growth inhibitors and it is sold as a shrub reaching no more that 60cm/2ft high. The plant will live for 4 or 5 years as an indoor plant before becoming too straggly and losing its vigour. Even so, pruning is necessary to encourage further flowering after new growth appears and to keep the plant in check; cut back up to half the previous year's growth. *Clerodendrum* flowers on new growth and the weak stems will need to be supported.

Keep it in a cool place during winter as it cannot cope with heating units or air conditioning.

Clerodendrum thomsonae can look striking in a hanging basket but it is important to pinch out the stem tips to prevent legginess

PROBLEMS

If the air is too dry, flowers and buds can drop off. Keep the air around the plant humid by spraying.

If the plant does not flower, the humidity and temperature must be increased during the growing period.

Spray with a systemic insecticide if the plant is infested with whitefly. White woolly patches on the axils of leaves indicate mealy bug. Spray with diluted malathion.

CARE

Light and temperature
Very bright, but no direct sun. It needs warmth and humidity. Allow it to rest during winter when it loses it leaves.

Water and feeding
Clerodendrum likes warm soft water. Do not let the plant dry out and feed once a week from spring to autumn with a high-nitrogen fertilizer. Make sure there is plenty of humus in the compost at all times, and if possible stand the pot over a tray of moist pebbles.

Propagation
This plant is difficult to propagate and requires a heated propagator if the 10cm/4in cuttings taken in spring are to grow. Dip them in hormone rooting powder and allow 6–8 weeks for new growth to appear.

Repotting
Every spring, cut back and pot on in good peaty compost which has had plenty of leafmould worked into it.

Clivia miniata (Kafir lily)

EASY

From Natal in South Africa, this rhizome develops heads of between 8–10 pretty orange bell-shaped flowers from thick stalks surrounded by glossy leaves. Varieties with red, yellow or cream flowers may occasionally be found as indoor plants.

A subtropical plant originally, it grows amongst rocks and crevices in damp and shaded conditions. It reaches 45cm/1.5ft in height and will flower regularly in early spring, but only when certain rules are obeyed: it needs space, winter rest and does not like to be repotted unless it is absolutely bursting out. Remove the dead flower stalk. The plant will benefit from a spell outdoors during the summer months.

Clivia lives for many years and is a striking plant.

Clivia miniata

CARE

Light and temperature
Bright light, but no direct sun, and cool or average warmth. Keep at a temperature of 8°C/50°F through the dormant period and at room temperature in summer.

Water and feeding
Water moderately in summer but hardly at all in winter. Always ensure good drainage. As soon as the flower stalk emerges from the base of the plant, feed on a weekly basis with general liquid fertilizer until the end of summer. Mist the leaves frequently.

Propagation
In early spring separate young offshoots after flowering with a sharp knife, ensuring the young plant retains its roots. Several growing in the same pot look attractive. The offsets may take 2 or 3 years to flower.

Repotting
Do this only when essential. Established plants only require the top 8cm/3in of soil to be changed using a soil-based compost.

PROBLEMS

White woolly patches on leaves indicate mealy bug. Remove with a swab dipped in methylated spirit.

If leaves become brown and scorched, move the plant out of the sun and do not water in direct sunlight.

Flowers may fall prematurely, in which case move to a cooler position.

If no flower spike appears once the plant has reached maturity, wait a further year and allow a longer winter resting period. Ensure correct watering takes place during the growing phase.

Cyclamen persicum (Alpine violet, florist's cyclamen)

QUITE DIFFICULT

This is, deservedly, among the most popular of all flowering plants. In full bloom it is glorious in winter time, with beautiful flowers in a range of colours on long stalks above big heart-shaped leaves in variegated shades of green and silver.

Originally from the Mediterranean region, cyclamen corms grow in poor alkaline soil and in rock crevasses, and like dappled light in semi-shaded conditions. The varieties available commercially have often been forced into flower and can drop dead on you: buy only from a trusted source and never a plant that looks droopy. It likes cool conditions and a north-facing windowsill is ideal. Alpine violets, as the name suggests, can withstand slight frosts and may be planted in window boxes, where they will keep throughout the winter in temperate zones.

There are 3 main varieties, each coming in many different shades of pink, red, white and purple. Some have contrastingly coloured 'eyes'. *Cyclamen persicum* has a height and spread of 30cm/12in. The original species had a delicate scent, but this, sadly, has been bred out of modern plants. New scented varieties are currently being introduced.

The intermediate variety grows to a height and spread of 25cm/9in. It is compact and fast-growing, often bearing more than 30 flowers at a time.

The miniature varieties reach only 15cm/6in or less and bear dainty flowers in a wide range of colours. The 'Puppet' and 'Kaori' series have slightly scented flowers.

Most cyclamens are discarded after a few weeks, but with the right care and attention, they can bloom for up to 2 months in winter, and be kept going for a few years. However it is not worth much effort in trying to recover a plant that has been severely stressed by over- or underwatering.

CARE

Light and temperature
A bright but not sunny spot, airy but not too warm. Optimum winter temperatures are around 15°C/60°F: In summer, when the plant is dormant, place it outside in a semi-shaded position. Good air circulation helps.

Water and feeding
Keep the plant moist but not wet. In summer, reduce water intake. *Cyclamen* is very sensitive to too much water, which is the most common cause of its collapse. Water by standing in a bowl of water at room temperature and then allow to drain thoroughly. Never water the top of the corm where the leaves and flower stalks are clustered. Feed weekly before and during flowering. Pull out old leaves and flowers, as the old stalks rot quickly and

this rot can spread to the rest of the plant. Do not spray flowers as this may cause them to become spotted, but give the plant adequate humidity.

Propagation
Sow from seed in late summer at 18–20°C/ 64–70°F using a heated propagator. Cover the seeds with soil and pot up when germinated. Give young plants a lot of light. Most varieties will take up to 18 months to flower, but the miniature varieties take only half that length of time.

Repotting
In midsummer when the old leaves die back, repot using fresh compost – up to half of the corm should be above soil level – and stand the pot in a cool but bright position.

Cyclamen persicum

PROBLEMS

Too much hot dry air causes the leaves to yellow. Other causes may be too little water or too much sunlight.

If the plant collapses and rots, the cause is likely to be overwatering. Allow it to dry out. Never water the corm.

Shortened blooming periods can be the result of too much warm dry air and insufficient fertilizer.

Minute cyclamen mites may infect the plant, causing curled leaf edges, stunted leaves and withered buds. This pest flourishes in humid conditions and all infected leaves must be destroyed. Insecticide is of no use.

Lack of sunlight and too much heat may cause new leaves to have very long, weedy stems and will discourage new flowers.

Columnea (Goldfish plant)

DIFFICULT

Columnea

Columnea gloriosa is one of the most striking of all hanging plants, with long green tendrils producing red, orange and scarlet tubular-shaped flowers which appear at various times of the year. It is, of course, ideal for a conservatory where its glorious shape can be shown off to good effect. Its natural habitat is Central America, mainly in the dense jungles of Costa Rica, and it was named after the sixteenth-century Italian botanist, Fabius Columna.

Columnea gloriosa has trailing stems with hairy leaves and grows to 90cm/36in or more, while the hybrid *Columnea stavanger* has smooth leaves on stems which grow to the same length. *Columnea banksii* is one of the most commonly available and is also one of the easiest to make do well.

But be warned – it is a fussy plant that requires constant attention, most importantly high humidity and an enforced period of rest during winter. It will do well for 3 or 4 years and should then be replaced with new plants.

C. banksii   *C. gloriosa*

CARE

Light and temperature
Bright light, but not direct sunshine. It does not like temperatures to fall below 13°C/55°F and will take up to 24°C/75°F as long as there is good humidity. The foliage will scorch if it touches the hot glass of a window.

Water and feeding
Columnea needs frequent, often daily, misting, but do not spray in direct sunlight otherwise the flowers may scorch. Avoid hard water and alkaline fertilizers. During summer, keep the soil moist but not wet, otherwise root rot or botrytis will set in. In winter keep the soil slightly damp, almost dry. Feed weekly in summer with a weak solution of liquid fertilizer. If possible, stand the plant on a bed of moist pebbles to provide a humid atmosphere.

Propagation
Use a heated propagator and take cuttings when the flowering season ends. Dip them in rooting hormone powder and plant into a rich compost of sand and loam. Make sure the cuttings are not allowed to dry out. They should take in about 3 weeks.

Repotting
Repot every 2 years after blooming into a humus-rich compost.

PROBLEMS

If the trailers become straggly, prune them by about half their length after flowering to encourage bushiness.

Draughts and central heating will cause leaves to drop. Spray the foliage daily with lime-free water.

Red spider mite can attack this plant. Treat with a systemic insecticide and then improve the humidity of the plant to prevent further attacks.

If flowers fail to appear, move the plant to a brighter spot.

Dipladenia sanderi (Rose dipladenia, pink allamande)

QUITE DIFFICULT

This sturdy little climber, also known as *Mandevilla sanderi*, bears pretty purple, dark red or white flowers all summer long. Unchecked, it can reach 3m/10ft or more, but pruned or trained around a frame it is a much smaller bushier plant. It grows fast and is rewarding, the flowers appearing on the current season's growth. It should be pruned back strongly after flowering to encourage new blooms the following year.

From tropical Brazil, where it climbs on neighbouring undergrowth in very humid conditions, *Dipladenia sanderi* is one of the most readily available hybrids and has either pink (*D. s. rosea*) or strong red (*D. s. rubiniana*) flowers. A newer variety is the scented *Dipladenia boliviensis*, which bears white flowers with yellow throats.

This plant is extremely poisonous, both leaves and flowers, and for this reason it has never been very popular.

CARE

Light and temperature
Bright light or semi-shade, but not direct sun. *Dipladenia* likes to be very warm and humid all year round, with temperatures never lower than 15°C/60°F. Fresh air circulation is important.

Water and feeding
Water twice a week with soft tepid water but make sure the soil has dried out first and feed every fortnight during flowering. After blooming, reduce the amount of water and rest the plant from autumn through to spring. Keep humidity at a reasonably high level.

Propagation
In spring, take tip cuttings. These can be successfully rooted with the aid of hormone rooting powder using a heated propagator. Good drainage is important. The plantlets should take in around 3 weeks.

Repotting
Repot only when potbound, or if it fails to produce new growth, using good houseplant compost mixture.

PROBLEMS

Leaves will curl and wither if the air is too dry and the plant will not flourish if its roots are cold and wet.

The leaves will also go yellow if given low humidity in summer. Stand the pot on a tray of moist pebbles.

Whitefly and red spider mite can sometimes attack. Spray with insecticide.

Mealy bug causes white cotton wool patches on the axils of the leaves. Spray with diluted malathion or rub off with cotton wool swabs dipped in alcohol.

Dipladenia sanderi. In Greek *diploos* means 'double' and *aden* 'gland', referring to the glands in the flower's ovary

Echeveria (Firecracker plant, moulded wax, hen and chickens, painted lady)

QUITE EASY

This succulent plant belongs to the cacti family and makes a perfect houseplant as it thrives on the dry hot atmosphere created by central heating. Give it a good rest period during the winter.

Originally from the desert areas of Mexico and the southern states of the US, *Echeveria* forms rosettes of leaves which are fleshy and covered with a 'bloom' that can be easily damaged. The bell-shaped flowers last only a day or so, but the plant itself is extremely long lived.

CARE

Light and temperature
Plenty of direct sunlight will please this plant – a south-facing windowsill, with spells on the sunniest patio during the summer months. For the rest period keep in temperatures as low as 10°C/50°F.

Water and feeding
Water sufficiently to prevent the soil drying out in the rest period; only sparingly during the growth and flowering months. Flat varieties that cover the soil can be watered by standing the pot in 5cm/2in of water for 30–60 minutes; drain well. Feed with cactus fertilizer on a weekly basis when the plant is growing.

Propagation
Remove offsets or take leaf cuttings in spring. Leave them to dry out for a week or so then pot up in sandy compost. Rooting will occur in 2 weeks, provided watering is only just sufficient to keep compost from drying out.

Repotting
Do this in spring into a shallow pot one size larger. Good surface drainage is important so work in some sand.

PROBLEMS

Overwatering will lead to rot and the production of soft leaf growth at the expense of flowers. Cut out rot and water less often.

Scorched leaves – do not allow water to remain on the leaves.

Dry brown spots on the leaf indicate underwatering. Increase watering, particularly in summer.

Mealy bugs find the close-set leaves perfect. Use a brush dipped in denatured alcohol to remove each bug individually.

Echeveria pumila

Echeveria agavoides

Echeveria agavoides

Euphorbia pulcherrima (Poinsettia, Christmas star, Mexican flame leaf)

DIFFICULT

In its native Mexico, the tropical *Euphorbia pulcherrima* often climbs to 3m/10ft or more. It flowers when the days are shortest, hence our ability to adapt it to indoors. The Americans were instrumental in developing the plant during the 1960s, from the original which was first recorded in 1834. Today we prepare over 7 acres of poinsettias for sale into the Christmas trade.

The plant grows only to about 45cm/1½ft. The flowers, which are really coloured bracts, make a wonderful show in cream, yellow, pink or red and should last for 2–3 months. There are single-stemmed or standard forms available commercially. 'Pulcherrima' means 'the most beautiful'.

Most people treat this plant as an annual and throw it away after flowering so never buy a specimen whose leaves are falling. It is difficult, but not impossible, to make it flower again. Pinch out the growing tips to help the plant become bushy.

To achieve flowers for a second year, cut off the stems to about 8cm/4in above the pot when the leaves have fallen. Place it in a mild shady spot and let the compost dry off. In early May, water and repot. Keep watering and shoots will soon reappear. Feed regularly and prune the new growth to leave 4 or 5 strong stems.

Lighting then needs to be very carefully controlled from the end of September. The plant must be in complete darkness for 14 hours each day, so you must cover it with a black polythene bag or something similar. Do this for 8 weeks and then bring it into the light and start watering. Nursery men use a growth retardant to limit the size and bushiness of the poinsettia but this is not often on sale at garden centres.

CARE

Light and temperature
Bright light during winter and a minimum temperature of 13–15°C/55–60°F. The plant must be protected from hot summer sun if it is to flower again next Christmas.

Water and feeding
These plants need moist air, so spray frequently. Water well and wait until the compost is thoroughly dry before watering again. Water more liberally in summer or if leaves begin to wilt. Feed weekly from early summer to mid-autumn.

Propagation
Take a stem cutting in early summer. Using a rooting hormone powder, plant the cuttings in small peat pots in a propagator, having been treated in water to stem the milky white juices. They will take in 3 or 4 weeks.

Repotting
Pot on in fresh peat when new growth is evident. Keep the pot the same size to encourage flowering rather than leaf growth.

PROBLEMS

Red spider mite and mealy bug are the main pests and can be sprayed with insecticide.

Overwatering causes the leaves to fall off after wilting. Make sure the compost is dry before you water.

If the temperature is too low, or there is not enough light, leaves will fall without wilting.

Eustoma grandiflorum (Prairie gentian)

DIFFICULT

In the garden or in its native habitat of Central America, this incredibly beautiful plant, with scented violet, pink and cream bell-shaped flowers, grows to 90cm/36in and until recently was sold only as a cut flower known as *Lisianthus russelianus*. It is particularly popular in Europe.

Today nursery men use growth inhibitors to produce plants about a third of the size that are suitable for indoor cultivation. They have lovely blue-green oval leaves and, with the right care and attention, should flower for up to a month. There are usually 2 or 3 plants in a pot. Discard after flowering.

Eustoma grandiflorum

CARE

Light and temperature
No direct sunlight but extremely bright and warm conditions.

Water and feeding
Water moderately and feed each week until the blooms are spent.

Propagation
This is best left to professionals, although the plant can be raised from seed in early summer using a heated propagator. The seedlings should be kept in a bright position, at temperatures of 15–18°C/60–64°F. A year after the seed is sown, plants should begin to flower.

Repotting
Not needed if the plant is discarded after flowering.

PROBLEMS

If the plant is in a draught, it will wilt immediately and not recover.

The plant will wilt, too, if overwatered. Never allow the roots to become soggy.

Creamy white

Pink

Double

Exacum affinae (German, Persian, Mexican or Arabian violet)

EASY

The German violet, a member of the gentian family, has tiny, glossy leaves and produces countless white or purple scented flowers in summer through to autumn. It is a small plant, reaching a height of 15–20cm/6–8in, with a spread of about the same. Also available is a pretty double species, *Exacum affinae rokokko*.

It is a biennial from the Socotra Island in the Gulf of Aden, and away from its native habitat is best raised from seed or bought as an indoor plant as it often withers after flowering. Plant in a shallow container about 12cm/4in in diameter. Pick off dead flowers to prolong the flowering season and if attempting to overwinter the *Exacum*, prune it back hard at the end of the flowering period to maintain its bushy character.

Exacum affinae rokokko

Exacum affinae 'Persian Violet'

CARE

Light and temperature
A very bright position, but no full midday sun. Average warmth and good air circulation are important for success.

Water and feeding
Always keep compost moist, never soggy. If the rootball dries out, the flowers will fade and quickly die. Feed once a fortnight and pinch off faded flowers. Keep the pot on a tray of moist pebbles if possible.

Propagation
From seed sown in early winter on the surface of a sphagnum-rich compost, and leave the seed uncovered. The seedlings will flower the following spring and should be potted up in a rich compost with good drainage.

Repotting
Overwintered plants should be repotted in early spring into pots one size larger, using a humus-based compost.

PROBLEMS

The *Exacum* will wilt immediately if placed in a draughty situation.

If flowers fail to form, move to a brighter position and ensure the plant has sufficient humidity.

Fuchsia

QUITE DIFFICULT

Fuchsia is one of the most popular flowering shrubs. Some hybrids can grow as tall as 2m/6ft outdoors, but inside the most suitable are dwarf or hanging varieties. There are certainly many to choose from, with flowers in almost every colour except yellow.

The plant blooms from March through to November, bearing highly ornamental bell-shaped flowers on stems that have small pointed deciduous leaves.

In summer, plants that are normally kept indoors will thrive if given short spells outside in bright light, but not direct sun. Buy small specimens in spring and place the pots in holders filled with wet gravel to increase humidity. In winter, though the leaves will drop, the plant will remain dormant if kept in a cool room.

Fuchsia's original habitat is New Zealand and Central America, where it grows to tree size in full sun.

Fuchsia 'Golden Marinka'

Fuchsia 'Marinka', a red hanging type

Fuchsia 'Lena', one of the many doubles

Fuchsia 'Winston Churchill', a single hybrid

CARE

Light and temperature
A bright position, but not full sun, with temperatures of 15°C/60°F in summer and 8–10°C/46–50°F in winter.

Water and feeding
Fuchsias like humidity, so spray often. Water plentifully throughout flowering and feed once a week. When the plants are not in flower, feed each fortnight. In winter allow the plant to dry out between waterings.

Propagation
Cuttings from the tips can be rooted in spring or autumn and set in a heated propagator.

Repotting
As necessary, in a potting mixture made of loam, peat and sand in equal parts. Hanging varieties need to be pruned by two-thirds in spring and repotted when new shoots appear.

PROBLEMS

Aphids and whiteflies can infest the plant. Spray with insecticide.

Leaves turn yellow and drop if the plant becomes waterlogged. Allow to dry out before watering again and ensure good drainage.

Gardenia jasminoides (Common gardenia, Cape jasmine)

DIFFICULT

The scent of a single *Gardenia* bloom can permeate an entire room and it is for this characteristic that the plant is memorable. It is difficult to grow indoors, because it needs high temperatures and high humidity to flower. Therefore it is best regarded as a greenhouse or conservatory plant which is brought indoors when in flower. However the one thing *Gardenia* hates most is a change of environment, which will cause buds to drop and the tips of new growth to blacken – so beware!

Originally from China, there are over 60 known species (named after the American botanist Alexander Garden), but the most generally cultivated here is *Gardenia jasminoides*, which was introduced into England in 1754, and into the US 45 years later.

It is a pretty plant, with attractive glossy dark green leaves and white single or double flowers which bruise easily and fade to creamy yellow before dropping. Nursery men have cultivated double forms of *Gardenia jasminoides*, which have superb scent.

The plant can grow up to 120cm/4ft high and wide, but only at a rate of 15cm/6in a year. It is best discarded after 4–5 years.

CARE

Light and temperature
Bright light, but always away from direct sunlight in summer. To flower, it needs summer temperatures of 15–18°C/60–64°F and, ideally, no fluctuations of temperature between night and day. In winter, it can survive at 12°C/55°F while resting.

Water and feeding
Gardenia needs to be watered frequently in summer. It likes high humidity and should be stood on a tray of moist pebbles at all times. A bright bathroom windowsill is ideal when the plant is indoors. In winter, water less and always use tepid rain water. Feed once a fortnight with half-strength fertilizer and spray regularly, avoiding the flowers, as this causes them to mark and discolour.

Propagation
Young stem cuttings can be taken in early spring and placed in a sand and loam compost in a heated propagator at a temperature of 18–21°C/64–70°F.

Repotting
As necessary when the plant outgrows the pot.

PROBLEMS

Mealy bugs, scale insects and spider mites can attack the plant. Spray with insecticide, and try to find ways of increasing the humidity to deter further attacks.

Yellowing leaves indicate either too little light, or chlorosis from using water with a high lime content. Water with sequestered iron and use only lime-free water or rain water.

If the flower buds drop before opening the plant needs more humidity. Spray daily with soft and tepid water, avoiding the flowers.

Gardenia hates draughts and a change in conditions. Avoid gas fumes at all times.

Gardenia jasminoides is a rewarding plant if kept free from temperature changes

Gerbera jamesonii (African daisy, Transvaal daisy, Barbeton daisy)

EASY

Gerbera jamesonii has lobed leaves which are woolly on the undersides. The long-lasting flowers are most often flame-coloured but may be shades of salmon-pink, yellow or white

CARE

Light and temperature
As bright as possible, with 3–4 hours of sun. The plant needs good air circulation with a summer temperature of up to 21°C/70°F.

Water and feeding
Keep the compost moist and feed once a week during flowering.

Propagation
From seed, sown in early spring and potted on into 14cm/5in pots. Most hybrids flower well in the first year of sowing but the flower stems from home-grown seeds revert to the longer, somewhat ungainly length.

Repotting
Not necessary as *Gerbera* is discarded after flowering.

PROBLEMS

Negligible, as the flower is an annual.

Gerbera is one of the most popular summer pot plants. Its major attraction is its showy, large, daisy-shaped flowers which come in unusual and subtle colours. There are double as well as single forms, although most people agree the latter are more graceful. It is also popular as a cut flower.

    Gerbera jamesonii is a perennial from the Transvaal, where it grows in full sun, rooting itself in rocky crevasses. The flowers are long-lasting, which is part of its attraction, and the flower stems are up to 60cm/2ft in length. Nursery men have bred an indoor plant variety, which is generally regarded as an annual, but this has stems around half the length. Buy plants in bud in early summer.

    New varieties have now been bred from tissue culture giving up to 6 blooms at a time, with the foliage less vegetative than before.

Gloriosa rothschildiana (Glory lily, climbing lily, Mozambique lily)

EASY

Gloriosa rothschildiana is a tuber which originates from tropical East Africa and is part of the lily family. It is a vigorous climber, reaching over 2m/7ft in height, and in its native habitat it will quite happily clamber over other plants and trees. It has glossy leaves, the uppermost ones formed as tendrils which makes this an interesting plant even when the flowers are not out.

The stunning red flowers, veering towards orange at the base, have 6 petals with wavy edges that curve inwards. There are some entirely yellow varieties.

The plant blooms from June to August each year, but in a greenhouse can be forced to flower from February onwards. Rest periods are important. It should last a good few years – perhaps 6–8 – with the right conditions. The tubers contain poison.

It is a plant that is now becoming much more widely available.

CARE

Light and temperature
Gloriosa needs as much light and direct sunshine as possible. Its favourite temperature is 15–18°C/60–64°F. Protect the flowers from sun and scorching on very hot days.

Water and feeding
Water abundantly during growth and put the pot over a saucer of wet gravel. Feed with a weak solution of liquid fertilizer each fortnight. After flowering, allow the plant to dry out between each watering until it finally withers. Cut back all vegetation to just above soil level and cease watering. Place the pot in a dark spot and keep dry. Do not allow the temperature to drop below 8°C/48°F, then repot tubers into fresh compost in early spring.

Propagation
In early spring, separate the small tubers which have formed among the roots of the parent plant. These can be potted out and left to develop green buds at 15–18°C/60–64°F.

Repotting
Each year. In winter the parts of the plant above ground die off and the tubers should be kept at 10–12°C/50–54°F. In early spring repot these tubers in a mixture of loam, peat and sand mixed in equal parts. Each tuber will produce 3 stems, which need support.

PROBLEMS

Uneven temperatures and a drop in humidity may cause dark spots to appear on the leaves. Keep both constant.

Leaves may wilt if the temperature is too high.

If flowers fail to appear, move to a sunnier position and ensure the right degree of humidity.

Gloriosa rothschildiana is a climber with weak stems needing support. Also found is *Gloriosa superba* that has green and orange flowers fading to red.

Heliotropium arborescens (Heliotrope, cherry pie)

EASY

This flowering herb from Peru gives off a delicious vanilla scent from its tiny flowers which are borne on large heads. Its flowering season is throughout the summer, when the perfume can be easily and deliciously detected in any room. It is a simple plant to grow and can be trained as a standard.

In its native habitat and with sufficient humidity *Heliotropium* will grow into a large shrub. As an indoor plant it can reach up to 1m/3ft high and will live for many years, but it will lose its ability to produce flowers over time. The most commonly available are the purple varieties, but white- or blue-flowering heliotropes may be found.

CARE

Light and temperature
Plenty of light but no direct sun. Average warmth in summer and temperatures of not less than 8–10°C/40–50°F in winter.

Water and feeding
Keep the compost well watered in spring and summer but never allow the plant to become waterlogged. Feed at weekly intervals using a general liquid fertilizer to manufacturer's recommendations. Whilst dormant, allow the plant to dry out between waterings and do not feed.

Propagation
From seed in early spring or from cuttings taken in late spring or summer and rooted in seeding compost in a propagator at 21°C/70°F.

Repotting
Heliotropium thrives best if repotted each spring. Use a humus-rich compost and a pot one size larger.

PROBLEMS

Scale insects on the underside of leaves should be treated by using a swab dipped in methylated spirit.

Aphids can infest the plant. Spray with diluted malathion.

Thrips can cause the leaves to lose their colour and develop flecks. Spray with diluted malathion.

Heliotropum arborescens, sometimes known as *H. peruvianum* has attractively wrinkled leaves

Hibiscus rosa-sinensis (Chinese hibiscus)

EASY

Hibiscus plants look particularly pretty on windowsills where their large flowers with long yellow stamens can bloom almost continuously all summer.

The trumpet-shaped flowers only last a day or two, but given the right care and attention you can achieve a succession of blooms over a few months. The flowers are large and measure up to 15cm/6in across. They can be double or single, in shades of yellow, orange, pink or red.

In its native habitat of tropical Asia and Southern China, the plant grows up to 3m/10ft tall in full sunshine, but indoors generally it reaches a height of around 1m/3ft.

Hibiscus can live for 20 years or more but needs to be pruned to keep it small and bushy. It can also be trained as a standard.

Hibiscus rosa-sinensis

CARE

Light and temperature
Very bright to full sun throughout summer. Warm temperatures during the flowering season. In winter, temperatures of around 15°C/60°F help promote the development of flowers in the next season.

Water and feeding
Water daily throughout summer until autumn, less in winter. From spring to autumn, feed each week; in winter, feed each month. *Hibiscus* must be fed otherwise it will not bloom.

Propagation
From top cuttings in late spring. Pot in fresh compost and keep moist and warm.

Repotting
Young plants need to be repotted each year. Older plants as necessary. Before repotting, cut back long shoots.

PROBLEMS

Dry compost will cause buds to drop.

Leaves will curl if the air is too dry.

Aphids and red spider mite can cause problems. Spray with insecticide.

Hoya bella (Miniature wax plant, porcelain flower)

EASY

Hoya bella is a delicate tropical plant, originally from India, where it grows in rocky crevasses and in the forks of tree trunks under leaf canopy. The scented flowers are star-shaped and pure white with pink and purple centres. They develop throughout the summer months and the plant flowers more profusely if it is not pruned.

Rather more robust is *Hoya carnosa*, a native of subtropical China and Australia, sometimes known as the honey plant because of its nectar-like smell. It climbs vigorously and has pale creamy pink flowers with crimson centres. It can grow quite easily to a height of 3m/10ft. A variegated form can sometimes be found on sale. It is a shy flowerer.

Hoya bella lives for up to 5 years, though *Hoya carnosa* can be kept going for much longer.

CARE

Light and temperature
Keep the plant out of strong midday sun but give up to 4 hours of direct sun each day. Because of its tropical origins, it needs to be kept warm, around 16–21°C/60–70°F.

Water and feeding
Water often during summer and sparingly when the compost dries out in winter, preferably with rain water. Feed during spring and summer with general houseplant liquid fertilizer, at half strength, on a fortnightly basis.

Propagation
Stem or tip cuttings can be taken from mature shoots, dipped first in hormone rooting powder, and planted in a rich humus-based compost in a propagating frame.

Repotting
Repot in spring when the plant has outgrown its pot into loam-based compost to which a little sand and polystyrene granules have been added. Cut back leggy stems.

PROBLEMS

Mealy bugs and aphids sometimes infest the plant and need to be sprayed with insecticide.

Too much water and cold roots cause the leaves to drop and the stems to die back.

If its position is too dark, the flowers and buds will drop. Move to a brighter spot.

If flowers do not appear, increase fertilizer cautiously. Overfeeding can cause leaf and stem development rather than flowering.

There are up to 12 flowers in a cluster of *Hoya bella*

Hydrangea macrophylla (Hydrangea)

EASY

Hydrangea macrophylla has a short life indoors, of around 6 weeks, but makes a lovely spring or summer outdoor plant, because once its glorious mop heads of blooms are finished it can be planted in the garden, where it will survive for many years. If you want it to flower again the following year as a houseplant, put it into a greenhouse with good light.

The plant comes from Japan and was introduced into Europe in 1790. Its flowers are naturally pink, but will turn blue when watered with aluminium sulphate. There is also a white variety. The recent 'lacecap' varieties are beautifully delicate, with some florets opening on the flower head while the inner ones are still in bud.

Choose plants that are in bud and which have strong healthy foliage with no broken stems. Never allow the roots to dry out.

CARE

Light and temperature
As much light as possible, but not direct sun. When in flower, normal room temperature is quite adequate unless above 18°C/64°F. In winter, the plant prefers a temperature of 7°C/45°F, which should be raised to 13°C/55°F in February for spring flowers.

Water and feeding
Hydrangea loves water and it does not hurt to immerse the pot in a bucket of water every second day. Feed once a week while flowering and in winter water only every 10 days or so. Blue varieties need lime-free water.

Propagation
Prune after flowering and cut the plant back to 2 pairs of new leaves. The tops of the prunings can be rooted in sand mixed with peat at temperatures of 13–16°C/55–61°F.

Repotting
Repot in damp compost at the end of the flowering season and place in the greenhouse.

PROBLEMS

Fungal infections, red spider mite and greenfly can infest these plants. Spray with fungicide for infections and insecticide for mites and greenfly.

Hydrangea macrophylla

Impatiens hawkeri hybrida

EASY

(Bizzie lizzie, patient Lucy)

The New Guinea *Impatiens*

Impatiens 'Blitz', the flowers of which are 5cm/2in across

Impatiens 'Sultani' variegata

CARE

Light and temperature
Bright to sunny position; the more sun the heavier the flowering. Good air circulation helps a lot. Room temperature throughout the year is fine. Never below 13°C/55°F.

Water and feeding
Water freely in summer, keeping the soil damp, but not wet; in winter, watering to prevent stem rot. *I. hawkeri* hybrids need humidity so stand over a tray of damp pebbles. Feed weekly throughout summer with a very weak dose of liquid fertilizer.

Propagation
Take tip cuttings of 5cm/2in long and root them in water. When the roots develop transfer to a rich potting compost. Seed can be sown in springtime.

Repotting
Clip back now and then to prevent plants from becoming straggly and leggy. You can repot in spring using potting mix, but unless the plant has retained its shape well it is better to start again.

PROBLEMS

Leaves may drop or wilt. The most common cause is underwatering. Immerse the pot for a good drink and allow it to drain thoroughly. Keep the compost moist, even if this means daily watering.

Flowers failing to form is usually a sign of lack of light – move to a sunnier position. Only repot when essential.

Red spider mite, aphids and whitefly can attack this plant. Treat appropriately.

Leggy growth often comes from warmth without sufficient light. Sunlight has increasingly become recognized as very important for success.

Until just after World War II, the bizzie lizzie was hardly known. Now it is one of the most common indoor plants, and is also used extensively for bedding outdoors during summer months. It is easy to propagate and children are often taught about plant life through taking cuttings of this colourful, fast-growing 'annual'. 'Tango', 'Red Magic' and 'Fanfare' are common examples.

A native of the tropical highlands of New Guinea, it was hybridized with several cultivars to produce the elliptically-leaved plants which will bloom throughout the year in the right conditions. The flowers range from reds and pinks to white. New breeding seeks to produce varieties with larger flowers.

The old-fashioned bizzie lizzie is *Impatiens walleriana*, coming originally from the spice island of Zanzibar, where it covers rocky surfaces and even roots itself in sandy beaches. 'Blitz' is probably the most pure of the reds. There is also a charming variegated form.

The name means impatient, and that it is. With regular attention success comes easily. After a year or two start again with fresh cuttings – the plant can go on much longer but will lose vigour.

Ixora stricta (Dwarf lemon)

QUITE DIFFICULT

Ixora, a member of the madder family, has never been hugely popular as an indoor plant. It is a tropical evergreen shrub, originally from Eastern Asia, where it thrives in humid and warm conditions as undergrowth in semi-shaded glades.

Ixora stricta, or *Ixora chinensis* as it is sometimes known, is a rounded plant with pretty pale yellow flowers which fade into shades of warm orange. Hybrids of *Ixora coccinea* (flame of the woods) and *Ixora javanica* (jungle geranium) are also commonly available and come in a range of colours, such as reds, oranges and pinks. The flower heads, which have flat tops and comprise many individual tubular flowers, appear from spring onwards, and over 4–5 years the plant will reach a height of 1.3m/4ft.

The leaves are quite glossy and thick, and are arranged in pairs. It is a bushy plant and the new foliage often has a bronze tinge, which matures to dark green.

Ixora is hungry for light and will do well if given the growing conditions it craves; otherwise there will be poor flowering and a lacklustre plant. It should not be subjected to cold water or cold draughts.

CARE

Light and temperature
This plant likes full sun on the windowsill. Direct sunlight is important for at least 5 hours a day, in temperatures which must not fall below 16°C/60°F.

Water and feeding
During the summer months, when *Ixora* is growing, feed every 2 weeks with a liquid fertilizer. Watering should be regular, though less frequent in dormant months. Use soft rain water at room temperature. The potting medium should be allowed to dry out before rewatering in winter.

Propagation
Cuttings are the best method, particularly if you have a propagating frame or can use artificial methods. Cut just below a leaf, with 8cm/3in of stem. Dip into a hormone rooting powder before potting into a mixture of peat, moss and sand. Place in the propagating frame at a constant temperature of at least 21°C/70°F. When the cutting has taken, acclimatize it slowly.

Repotting
Every spring for the first 4 years. Then just dig out the top 3cm/1in of soil and replace, using a mixture of peat, leafmould and sand.

PROBLEMS

Ixora is a tetchy plant; flower drop is caused by changes in temperature, as is leaf drop. Keep away from draughts and give the right amount of sun.

If the rootball is kept too moist or cold chlorosis may set it. Allow to dry out immediately and then water less frequently.

Scale insect can infest this plant. Treat with swabs of cotton wool dipped in methylated spirit.

Ixora stricta does not like changes in its conditions

Jasminum polyanthum (Pink jasmine)

QUITE EASY

Jasminum is a member of the olive family and needs a cool winter season followed by warmer temperatures to bring it into flower. It is a plant well worth keeping, for the flowers have a magnificent perfume, even if they are short lived. This is a vigorous grower, and can be trained on a hoop or allowed to romp in a conservatory.

Jasminum polyanthum comes from the Far East, where it grows in subtropical conditions, often to vast heights, scrabbling up other trees in wooded areas in semi-shady conditions. It was brought to Europe in the 1890s. The garden form of jasmine is *Jasminum officinal.*

The flowers have between 4 and 9 white petals which open from pinky buds in large clusters. There is always an odd number of leaves on the branches of this woody stemmed plant. Buy ones in bud and bring them on indoors in spring.

The plant will appreciate spending the summer months after flowering on a warm patio. Cut the plant back to half its size and pinch out growing tips to encourage side shoots to grow in order to produce a good compact plant for the following year.

Jasminum polyanthum

CARE

Light and temperature
The temperature is best kept at 13°C/55°F. In summer, when the plant is not flowering, it can rise to 21°C/70°F, but do not place it in direct sunshine. Good light is important.

Water and feeding
Water once every 4 or 5 days when flowering, using soft, tepid water. Feed fortnightly. When out of flower in summer water every second day. Resting the pot on a tray of moist pebbles helps humidity.

Propagation
Root stem-tip cuttings with at least 2 pairs of leaves taken in spring or autumn and set them at a temperature of 16°C/61°F, using a rooting hormone powder. They should take within 21 days.

Repotting
In spring after flowering, when potbound. But more usually these plants are regarded as annuals and if you do not have a conservatory or greenhouse, discard them. Older plants become straggly and woody after 4 or 5 years, at which time young cuttings can be brought on.

PROBLEMS

Red spider mite or greenfly can infest this plant. Spray with insecticide.

Dried up leaves indicate too little water. Follow the instructions in 'Water and feeding' carefully.

If the buds brown, the plant is too hot or too dry. Move to a cooler position, and increase the humidity by placing on a tray of moist pebbles.

If the buds fail to open the plant needs more light.

Kalanchoe blossfeldiana (Flaming Katie, Palm Beach belle)

EASY

Kalanchoe blossfeldiana is the most commonly found variety of this succulent, and indeed perhaps the most commonly sold houseplant. In its native Madagascar its bright red flowers appear during the winter, though Dutch breeders have manipulated hybrids which flower throughout the year, in colours from yellow and orange to pink and purple. It will appreciate a spell out of doors in a sunny sheltered spot in summer months, and can reach a height of 30cm/ 12in, though dwarf varieties are sometimes seen for sale.

Kalanchoe manginii is a spring-flowering type, demanding higher humidity, so stand on a tray of moist gravel and mist the leaves frequently. The flowers hang downwards, making good display of this plant important. 'Wendy' and 'Tessa' are just two of the many hybrids available.

CARE

Light and temperature
An east- or west-facing windowsill from spring to autumn and a south-facing windowsill in winter. It needs average warmth, with a minimum 10°C/50°F in winter. Remember these plants only develop flowers when they receive 8–10 hours of light each day for 4–6 weeks.

Water and feeding
Use high-potash fertilizer every 4 weeks during spring and summer. Water very sparingly during winter.

Propagation
Mostly done from seed sown in March or April. Leaf cuttings or whole shoots can be taken in spring and summer. Use a sharp knife and dust with hormone rooting powder. Either lay leaves or insert stems into a sand and peat compost.

Repotting
Best to do this straight after flowering if retaining the plant for a further season's flowering.

PROBLEMS

White woolly patches on leaves are caused by mealy bug. Remove with a methylated spirit swab.

Black patches on leaves can be removed by dusting the flowers with sulphur.

Wet and cold conditions cause leaves to drop and stems to become black. Dry the plant out.

Right: *Kalanchoe manginii* 'Tessa'

The fleshy leaves of *Kalanchoe* look a rich reddy-green in sunlight

Lantana (Yellow sage, shrub verbena)

QUITE EASY

Originating in the West Indies, this plant grows up to 2m/6ft and is a vigorous and fast-growing shrub, flowering throughout the year if it has sufficient light. Only dwarf hybrids are cultivated for indoor use. If left untrimmed, *Lantana* will reach 1.2m/4ft, but it is best pruned into a smaller, bushier shape. It can look good in a hanging basket.

It has pretty white, pink or yellow tubular flowers, which darken with age, on prickly stems that have rough leaves. It will bloom between May and October, but the only reliable indoor cultivar is *Lantana hybrida* 'Nana'. It should be discarded after 3–4 years.

CARE

Light and temperature
Lots of sunlight – it will not flower unless it gets 3–4 hours of direct sun each day throughout the year. It likes good air circulation and copes well with summer room temperatures. Rest in winter at about 10°C/50°F.

Water and feeding
Water freely while in flower and feed with liquid fertilizer each fortnight. In winter, allow the compost almost to dry out between waterings.

Propagation
From 10cm/4in cuttings taken from a non-flowering branch in August. Strip off the leaves, dip in rooting powder and plant in a mixture of peat and sand. Place in a greenhouse at 18°C/64°F, in bright but filtered light. Leave the cuttings over winter. In early spring, pinch the tips to encourage a bushy shape. In March, pot into standard growing soil.

Repotting
When potbound in compost made up of organic soil, sand and peat.

PROBLEMS

Lantana is very prone to whitefly. Spray with insecticide.

Lantana hybrida 'Nana'

Medinilla magnifica (Rose grape)

DIFFICULT

As the common name suggests, from March to June this bushy plant bears arching stems of drooping rose-pink flowers shaped like bunches of grapes and set in sensationally pretty pink bracts. The pairs of leaves have no stalks and measure up to 30cm/12in long and 12cm/5in wide. The stem of the plant is woody and has many branches.

Its native habitat is the tropical jungles of the Philippines, where it was discovered in 1888. There it grows to 2.5m/8ft, but as an indoor plant it reaches no more than 1m/3ft. It is difficult to make a success of indoors because it needs controlled temperature and humidity levels. Thus it is expensive. It is also best suited to a conservatory where it should last for a good number of years.

Medinilla magnifica

CARE

Light and temperature
In summer, it needs bright light but no direct sun. In winter it can take direct sunlight. It needs high temperatures of 18–27°C/64–80°F in summer. In winter it can tolerate 15–18°C/60–64°F when the plant is at rest, which is essential for further flowering.

Water and feeding
Water moderately, letting the soil almost dry out between waterings. In winter, water less. Humidity needs to be high and the foliage sprayed each day. The plant should be placed in a saucer of wet gravel. Feed with liquid fertilizer each fortnight from when buds form until September.

Propagation
Leave to the professionals.

Repotting
Every other spring in a compost made up of leaf mould, sphagnum moss, peat and sand. Pinch out tips of stems to encourage branching.

PROBLEMS

Prone to red spider mite. Spray with diluted malathion.

If flowers do not form, increase the difference in seasonal treatments, giving higher, more humid conditions in spring and cooler temperatures in the rest period.

Nertera granadensis (Bead plant, coral bead plant, baby tears)

QUITE EASY

This member of the madder family is a curious-looking but attractive low-growing creeping plant. Its fleshy green leaves intertwine to form a thick mat, with the whole plant growing no more than 7–8cm/3in high. Small white flowers are produced in June, followed by orangy-red berries covering the entire plant. These berries fall after a few months, and there are often so many of them that the foliage is hidden.

The native habitat of the bead plant stretches from the Andes to Cape Horn, New Zealand and Tasmania. It grows in high mountain zones at least 2000m/6500ft above sea level and so requires a lot of direct sunlight.

The plant is low, and should be grown in a container where the decorative berries can be displayed well.

CARE

Light and temperature
Needs 3–4 hours of direct sun a day, so a south-facing windowsill is ideal. However it requires cool temperatures of between 14–17°C/57–62°F. The plant will become straggly and refuse to bear fruit if it is placed in rooms which lack light or are too warm.

Water and feeding
Water thoroughly as needed, but let the surface soil dry out before repeating. Place the plant in a saucer of wet gravel. In winter reduce watering, but do not allow the plant to become completely dry. Feed only once a month, when the berries begin forming.

Propagation
In spring, divide clumps of old plants into 5 or 6 small portions and repot individually into fresh soil made up of peat, sand and organic mulch.

Repotting
Repot each year in spring when dividing.

PROBLEMS

Do not over-fertilize, or you will promote leaf growth rather than flowering.

If the flowers open but berries fail to form move to a better ventilated position.

Nertera granadensis is also sometimes sold as *Nertera depressa*.

Osteospermum (Trailing African daisy, Burgundy mound)

EASY

In its native habitat of the Cape and Natal province of South Africa, *Osteospermum* grows as ground cover and spreads easily. In the last year or so Danish nursery men have hybridized an indoor variety which is now marketed successfully throughout the summer months.

Its leaves have several points and are smallish. The cheerful flowers are a delicate purple fading to white on the upper side, with a deeper purple colour on the underside of the petals, the centres are dark purple. A most attractive and unusual plant, the flowering season lasts for 2 to 3 months. A white variety, *Osteospermum fruticosum* 'Album' is occasionally found on sale.

Osteospermum throws out long trailing branches which root easily, and can be cut and planted to increase stock. The plant will last for a couple of years but then loses vigour and is best replaced.

CARE

Light and temperature
Normal room temperature is fine; keep plant on a sunny, south-facing windowsill if possible, and give plenty of light during the winter months. Artificial light is not necessary.

Water and feeding
Keep the compost moist, but provide good drainage. Weekly watering in the winter rest period should be sufficient. Feed with a weak solution of houseplant fertilizer on a 7-day basis when in bud and flowering.

Propagation
Use the plantlets from the trailers and pot up into moist compost in spring. Water sparingly until new growth is obvious, then treat as a mature plant. Three or four months later flowering should commence.

Repotting
In early spring, into ordinary houseplant compost. Use a pot 1 size larger. This should only be necessary if trying to keep plant for a second season. Otherwise discard.

PROBLEMS

Whitefly needs to be treated with insecticide.

If plant becomes leggy, pinch out growing tips to encourage flowering and bushiness.

Osteospermum fruticosum

Orchids: Cymbidium hybrids

EASY   (Cymbidium orchids)

Orchids are probably the largest flowering plant family, with about 750 groups of *genera* and more than 30,000 species. The most spectacular of those cultivated as indoor plants are cymbidiums.

These orchids are native to tropical Asia and Australia, where they grow either in the forks of rainforest trees, on rocks (epiphytes) or on the ground (terrestrial).

As cut flowers they are long-lasting – up to 6 weeks – and can be found in a dazzling range of colours, from red and yellow, to pink, brown, green and white.

The leaves are tough and ribbon-shaped and when the plant produces long racemes of heavy waxy flowers, up to 30 per stalk, it makes a truly exotic display. Because most orchids available are grown in hothouses, they are usually available all year round. If you buy a plant with good healthy-looking buds, the flowers should bloom for up to 8 weeks, given the right care. The rhizomes like to be potbound.

The Victorian idea that orchids were hideously difficult to grow is no longer the case, particularly with cymbidiums, the easiest orchids to cultivate indoors. Two types are commercially available, the hybrids which grow to more than 1m/3ft tall and the miniature indoor cymbidiums which reach a height of around 60–90cm/2–3ft. The smaller varieties tolerate heated rooms best, and have flowers around 4–7cm/1½–3in across.

green hybrid with spotted lip

'Lemforde Surprise'

'Miniature Delight'

CARE

Light and temperature
Cymbidiums need a very airy, bright and sunny location and can be placed out of doors from early summer to early winter in a sheltered spot, but not full sun. Ensure plenty of contrast between warm daytime temperatures and cool night air when the buds are setting. A spell in a greenhouse where the orchid receives multi-directional light is helpful.

Water and feeding
Water from early spring to early autumn, but not too enthusiastically. It is best to let the compost dry out between waterings. Cymbidiums love humidity, so spray with water often and keep on trays of damp pebbles. Over 50 per cent humidity is needed for success. Feed with special orchid fertilizer every 4 weeks. Do not overdo feeding, as you will only produce more leaves at the expense of flowers.

Propagation
The easiest way is to divide the rhizome directly after flowering. Remove the plant from the pot, wash the roots thoroughly and cut through the rhizome with a sharp knife so you have 2 or 3 pseudobulbs (the bulbous fibrous growths at the bottom of the plant) and a fair clump of leaves on each new plant. Discard the dead growth. Water newly separated orchids sparingly, but spray well.

Repotting
Orchids, like most plants, like to be left alone and only need repotting every 2 or 3 years. The potting mixture should be one part sphagnum moss, one part organic soil, two parts of osmunda fibre and a pinch of bonemeal and charcoal. This mixture can be bought readily.

PROBLEMS

Scale insects and mealy bug can cause problems, so spray with an appropriate insecticide. It is advisable to wipe the leaves down each week.

Mildew on the leaves may be caused by over-misting in cool temperatures. Treat with fungicide and move to a warmer position.

Lighter leaves and those with yellow spotting indicate a viral disease for which there is no cure. Destroy the plant immediately.

Lack of flowers but vigorous growth of leaves indicates too little light.

Orchid phalaenopsis (Moth orchid)

DIFFICULT

These demanding plants are quite stunning during their long flowering period, which can last almost throughout the year. Several flower spikes can follow on after each other and the arching stalks carry many blooms. It is a pseudobulb, with fleshy light green leaves.

Many people fail with the moth orchid because it is very difficult to emulate the conditions in which the plant grows in its native habitat of Malaya.

A constant temperature is required – in summer 25°C/70°F and 16°C/60°F in winter. A cool night temperature helps. The difficulty of keeping the moth orchid at home is providing 10–15 hours light each day, so artificial light in winter is essential. The plants need no rest period. They can last for 4–5 years with the right care.

PROBLEMS

If the leaves shrivel and rot at the stem this may be caused by overwatering. Allow compost to dry out and reduce future waterings.

If the plant fails to produce new flower stalks, the most likely cause is insufficient light and humidity. Use artificial light if necessary and increase humidity.

Greenfly may attack this plant. Use insecticide before infestation becomes too serious.

CARE

Light and temperature
High temperatures by day and cooler at night is the secret of success with this plant. Place in a warm spot with as much daylight, but no direct sun, as you can manage.

Water and feeding
Humid conditions help enormously; stand the plant over a tray of damp pebbles if at all possible and spray the leaves often. Water weekly during flowering, ensuring the plant has good drainage.

Propagation
The moth orchid produces side bulbs, which may be separated from the parent plant. Remove the plant from the pot and delicately sort out the roots, washing thoroughly. Cut the bulb away if necessary with a sharp knife and pot up into specially prepared orchid compost which has been pre-moistened. The growth should start in 3–4 weeks. Water sparingly during that time.

Repotting
Only when absolutely essential if the plant is potbound, every 2 years or so. Use a special orchid compost, rich in sphagnum moss and osmunda fibre.

Pachystachys lutea (Lollipop plant)

QUITE DIFFICULT

The lollipop plant is often confused with *Beloperone* and was recently introduced into Europe as a variety of this plant. It does look similar, with its bright yellow bracts and long oval dark green leaves. The stems are erect and become woody with age. The bracts last for 3 months or more and from them emerge the 5cm/2in-long white flowers with green tops – these are very fresh but live for only a few days.

It comes from Peru, where it grows as a perennial. It can be kept going for a fairly long time but, in practice, 2–3 years will see it past its best.

Pruning is important to keep the plant from becoming straggly. In spring it will shoot again if cut back all over to 9cm/3in. Buy plants with well-leafed stems, particularly at the base – a lack of these leaves indicates it has been subjected to the wrong conditions.

CARE

Light and temperature
Full sun in summer; away from direct light in winter. The maximum summer temperature is 21°C/70°F. When resting keep in cooler condition but not less than 16°C/60°F or the lower leaves will fall.

Water and feeding
Keep well watered in summer. Do not allow the plant to become waterlogged. In winter, keep the soil just moist, allowing the topsoil to dry out before rewatering. Feed only in summer, every 14 days.

Propagation
In spring take young stem-tip cuttings from prunings. The cuttings should be about 8–10cm/3–4in long. Root them in sharp sand and peat, ensuring very good drainage, and place in a propagator at 18°C/64°F.

Repotting
Every spring, using new soil. The bigger the pot, the taller the plant will grow, and this may cause the lower stems to become deleafed and unattractive, so use a pot just one size up.

PROBLEMS

If the plant is allowed to dry out, the leaves will droop, then fall. Soak the pot, allow to drain thoroughly and water more regularly.

Lack of ventilation and humidity will cause the flowers to rot and drop off. Keep humidity constant by placing the plant in a saucer of wet gravel. Keep well ventilated.

If flowers fail to form apply a high-potash fertilizer for one season.

Pachystachys lutea

Passiflora caerulea (Blue passion flower)

QUITE EASY

The blue passion flower has a colourful background. It was named by Jesuit missionaries who discovered it growing in Brazil in the 1720s and likened its petals to the Ten Apostles who witnessed Christ's crucifixion. The anthers were the five wounds in Christ's side, the rays of the corona His crown of thorns, and the 3 stigmas represented the nails that pinned Him to the Cross.

The plant grows in tropical conditions, clinging by its tendrils to the trunks of other jungle trees. It will reach a height of 5m/16ft but is commonly sold as an indoor plant trained on a hoop.

The flowers of *Passiflora caerulea* are greeny-blue and purple. You may occasionally find *Passiflora violacea*, with its more pinkish flowers; this variety requires higher temperatures. It is a vigorous grower, which will go on for years. In a conservatory or greenhouse it should be grown in a close-fitting container as this will encourage flowering.

The passion flower needs heat, sun and ventilation to do well. It can be trained against an outdoor wall in a sheltered position or used with great effect in a hanging basket.

The intriguing flowers of *Passiflora caerulea* live for only for a day or so

CARE

Light and temperature
It needs bright light and 3 or 4 hours of sunshine each day. Bring it indoors for only a short time. It enjoys good ventilation and temperatures of around 21°C/70°F. Give the plant a good rest in winter at cooler temperatures.

Water and feeding
Water freely in summer and once a week or once a fortnight in winter. Feed every 2 weeks in summer during the growing season with liquid fertilizer at half strength.

Propagation
Cuttings of stem tips about 18cm/7in long can be rooted into pots of half sand and half peat moss at 21°C/70°F. Keep well sprayed until they begin to grow, which will be in 3 weeks time. Prune plants down to around 25cm/9in of the soil's surface each spring, despite the age of the plant.

Repotting
Passion flowers bloom best if their roots are restricted. Repot annually for the first year or two, then every spring add a fresh layer of compost to the surface. They will live for many years given the right conditions.

PROBLEMS

A lack of flowers means there is insufficient light. Move to a sunnier spot. If the leaf growth is strong yet no flower buds appear, reduce feeding.

Greenfly can infest the plant. Spray with insecticide.

Plumbago auriculata (Cape leadwort)

EASY

This South African perennial has light blue flower clusters or racemes which provide real joy in summer. In warmer climates, *Plumbago* is used as a particularly attractive hedge, or a cascading plant over walls and rockeries, where it grows with great vigour.

Indoors, it is best planted in a conservatory, where it can remain in a constant position, or in a narrow border, where roots have a freer spread than in a pot. It grows as much as allowed and needs its stems to be guided on some kind of support. It can live for many years. Cuttings take easily, so if the plant becomes straggly you should replace it. A white-flowered variety, *P. a. alba*, can be found.

Plumbago indica (scarlet leadwort) comes from South East Asia and is again a perennial in its native habitat. The zigzag stems are fascinating and the flowers a stunning shade of red. This plant is rarer to find for sale but is none the less rewarding and unusual.

Both varieties can do with pinching out the growing tips to encourage bushiness.

PROBLEMS

Young shoots can be attacked by aphids. Spray with fertilizer.

CARE

Light and temperature
Plumbago needs at least 3 hours of sunshine every day. It survives happily at room temperatures, but requires a rest in winter, preferably at around 10°C/50°F.

Water and feeding
Water regularly from spring to autumn, and feed every fortnight. In winter, reduce watering and let the soil dry out, though not completely. The plant appreciates a fertilizer high in potash during the growth period.

Propagation
In June or July, take 10cm/4in cuttings and plant in pots filled with a peat and sand compost. Cover with plastic bags and expose to filtered light. Uncover when rotting occurs.

Repotting
In early spring, move into a pot one size larger. Older plants can just have the top 5cm/2in of compost replaced with rich soil.

Plumbago auriculata used to be known as *Plumbago capensis*. It flowers on new growth

111

Pelargonium (Geranium)

EASY

Originally from the warmer areas of South Africa, *Pelargonium* was widely bred and hybridized by nursery men in the last century, since when nothing has diminished the plant's extraordinary international popularity.

It flourishes almost everywhere, happily tolerates dry atmospheres and is easy to grow from seed or from cuttings. It has no dormant period and modern hybrids will flower almost continuously for up to 10 months of the year, given ample light and sufficient water.

There are thousands of named varieties ranging from dwarf plants to standards of considerable height. The flowers come in shades of pink and red. Some have scented or variegated leaves and vary widely in shape and size. When buying, it is best to consult a specialist nursery catalogue.

Four of the biggest groups are zonal, ivy-leaf, regal and scented-leaf varieties. Many of the zonal geraniums (*P. x hortorum* or *P. zonale*) can be grown in pots for indoor use. The term 'zonal' comes from the leaf markings of most varieties, which are shaped like a horseshoe, giving the popular alternative name of 'horseshoe geraniums'.

Ivy-leaf varieties are classified as *P. peltatum* and have trailing stems with fleshy leaves. They can be trained along a trellis, or left to cascade from hanging pots or baskets. Indoors, they will flower most of the year if given good sunshine. There are over 200 varieties, including single, double and semi-double flowers. They are sometimes known as trailing pelargoniums.

Regal pelargoniums (*P. domesticum hybridus*) are often called just that and not geraniums. These have larger flower petals than other types and a plain green papery leaf. Indoors they will bloom for up to 9 months of the year, although older strains only flower for 2 months, so choose carefully. There are more than 1000 varieties of regal pelargonium, sometimes known as the Martha Washington pelargonium.

The main attraction of the scented-leaf varieties is the foliage, the flowers being rather insignificant. Leaves may be patterned in reds, browns, greens and yellows or have simple white or cream edgings. Their common names describe the different fragrances produced as the leaves are gently rubbed, ranging from nutmeg and ginger to apricot and lemon. The varieties are endless and breeders are working to make their flowers more dramatic.

Zonal pelargoniums

'Gazelle Ravenskeck'

'Frank Headley'

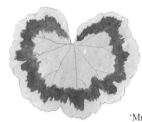

'Mrs Quilter'

'Mrs Henry Cox'

'Distinction'

Scented-leaf varieties

p. tomentosum
mint geranium

p. crispum
lemon geranium

p. x Fragrans variegatum

CARE

Light and temperature
Full light. It is a plant that is greedy for sun. Ordinary room temperature in summer, but no hotter than 24°C/75°F. In winter keep cooler at around 13–16°C/55–60°F.

Water and feeding
Water generously in summer, but keep almost dry in winter. Feed with liquid fertilizer each fortnight in summer. They like a dry atmosphere, so do not spray.

Propagation
By seed, or stem-tip cuttings taken in spring – both are easy. Seeds should be sown in spring at 16–18°C/60–64°F in sandy compost. Also in spring cut back by as much as a third; *P. x domesticum* can stand up to half. Always deadhead the plants.

Repotting
Pelargoniums like to be potbound, so only repot as they grow on from young cuttings.

regal

zonal

ivy leaf

cascade

PROBLEMS

A lack of flowers is caused by overfeeding, which encourages leaf growth at the expense of flowers. It may also be caused by too much winter heat.

Lack of light causes thin growth, and too little water causes the lower leaves to go yellow and develop brown patches. Ideally leaves should occur regularly and close together up the stems. Do not allow the plant to get leggy.

If pale yellow circles appear on the leaves, a virus has attacked the plant. Destroy the plant as there is no cure. Also fatal is black leg disease, where the stems blacken and rot near the soil's surface. This is caused by overwatering.

If a mass of distorted leaves begin to sprout, leafy gall disease is usually the problem. Again, there is no cure. Destroy the plant.

Geraniums are often infested with whitefly. Spray with malathion.

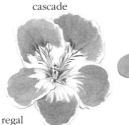

single

regal

'Stellar'

Primula (Primrose)

EASY

Primroses are perky little plants, useful for the colour and cheer they bring to the house. They come from the cooler regions of the Yunnan province of China and flower for up to 6 weeks, given the right conditions.

There are 4 varieties of *Primula*, which are perennial in their native habitat, growing under leaf canopy in wooded areas. However, when kept indoors they are usually treated as annuals.

Primula acaulis (or *P. vulgaris*) is a hybrid of the modern primrose, which comes from southern Europe, and is available in a wide range of colours.

Primula malacoides (the fairy or baby primrose) is naturally purple but also comes in bright pinks and whites as an indoor plant. It is very free-flowering in early spring, with large clusters of flowers on stems up to 15cm/6in high, sometimes producing additional tiers of flowers.

Primula obconica (the poison primrose) has round heart-shaped leaves, again with large flower clusters of up to 25cm/10in high. It comes in blue, white, apricot, red and crimson varieties. Some people are skin-sensitive to the leaves of this plant.

Finally comes P*rimula sinensis* (the Chinese primrose), which is smaller, with compact flower heads, and altogether more delicate.

CARE

Light and temperature
Plenty of light and sunshine in the morning and evening. Cool temperatures (10–15°C/50–60°F) will help to make the flowering season longer.

Water and feeding
Always keep the soil moist and feed with a half-strength dose of liquid fertilizer every 2 weeks or so while in flower.

Propagation
Seed can be sown up to the end of the summer in a propagator with the temperature set at 16°C/61°F. Once germination has taken place and the seedlings are established, pot up individually for flowering plants the following spring. Pick off dying flowers of the plant to encourage it to continue in flower in the hopes of producing seed.

Repotting
P. acaulis will move happily into the garden. *P. malacoides* may be repotted into a humus-rich compost to last for a second season and should then be discarded. Other primulas are best treated as annuals.

PROBLEMS

Primulas are prone to grey mould and red spider mite. Spray with fungicide and insecticide.

As soon as the leaves start to brown, cut them off with a sharp knife at the base of the plant.

Never allow the plant to droop as it will not recover fully. Keep the compost moist at all times, and ensure good drainage.

Primula obconica come in a multitude of colours

P. obconica

P. malacoides

P. acaulis

Rosa chinensis (Pygmy rose, China rose)

QUITE EASY

Rosa 'Judy Fisher', double flowered

Rosa 'Baby Darling'

Rosa chinensis

Although roses in all their beautiful and infinite varieties are undoubtedly the most popular of all garden plants, it is only over the last ten years that they have proved popular as indoor plants. This has been due to the introduction of new miniature varieties in Holland and Denmark where, with the use of artificial lighting, roses are available all year round, in a wide range of colours.

Roses are among the most ancient of cultivated plants and there are many varieties which will thrive in a conservatory, porch or garden room as long as there is adequate light, water and food. Of the new varieties, 'Parade' is one of the best plants for staying in flower longer. There are many variations of this plant – 'Royal Parade' (a beautiful pink), 'Fashion Parade' (a lighter shade), 'Victory Parade' (a red) and 'Dreaming Parade' (a soft salmon colour).

Rosa chinensis grows to around 30cm/1ft and, as its name suggests, originated in China.

CARE

Light and temperature
For summer blooms, bushes should be left outside and pruned severely in midwinter, then brought indoors to a well-lit position, with temperatures slowly increasing from 5°C/41°F to about 13°C/55°F over the next few months until spring. Roses need gradual acclimatization.

Water and feeding
The soil should always be moist, and once buds start to form liquid fertilizer should be added every 10 days. Spray the foliage. Stand over a tray of damp pebbles as high humidity promotes good health. After flowering, move them outdoors again.

Propagation
Through cuttings taken in spring, dipped in hormone rooting powder and potted in good rich potting mixture.

Repotting
Repot with fresh soil in autumn, but do not expect to do this more than 2 or 3 times. After that, move the plant permanently outdoors.

PROBLEMS

Roses are very suceptible to red spider mite and aphid infestation, and fungal diseases such as black spot. Watch carefully and spray with insecticide and fungicide when necessary. It is important to ensure good air circulation.

If the plant becomes leggy, encourage bushiness by pruning shoots back to just above growth buds that point away from the centre of the plant.

If the leaves curl up and look dry, underwatering is the cause.

Schlumbergera (Thanksgiving cactus, Christmas cactus, claw cactus)

QUITE EASY

In its natural habitat of tropical Brazil, this member of the cactus family is epiphytic, attaching itself on to trees that grow on mountains up to 1500m/4800ft.

Forced by hybridizing and the treatment meted out by nursery men, it is a strikingly attractive plant growing to about 30cm/1ft, and has stems formed of flat joints with a few well-marked 'teeth'. The flowers appear in winter and, for a cactus, are long-lasting – maybe 3 or 4 days. They are usually pink, but modern hybrids include white, red, yellow and purple varieties.

S. bridgesii is the Christmas cactus and *S. truncata* (sometimes known as *Zygocactus truncatus*) the Thanksgiving cactus, also called the claw cactus. They both come into flower in early November and can last for 50 years or more.

Schlumbergera bridgesii looks extremely handsome in a hanging basket or against plain terracotta pots.

CARE

Light and temperature
Some direct sun all year round. It does fine at room temperature. An abundance of flowers can be encouraged by keeping the plant out of artificial light for long periods during early autumn when buds are setting. An outdoor spell is recommended – a shady protected position in summer.

Water and feeding
Keep the soil moist but not wet, using rain water if possible. When flowering finishes, reduce the amount of water. Use high-potassium fertilizer every fortnight all year round except in the 2 months after flowering.

Propagation
In spring take cuttings of 2 to 3 joints, let the surface dry out and pot into a humus-rich compost. Rooting occurs in about 3 or 4 weeks.

Repotting
In spring, but only when roots fill the container. Use a mixture of leaf compost, soil, peat and sand, and keep dryish for the first 2 weeks.

PROBLEMS

Scale insects and mealy bug may infest the plant. Spray with insecticide.

If the plant shrivels up, it has probably been kept too dry. Increase watering and keep the compost moist.

If flowers fail to appear, the plant has been kept too warm during the rest period. Increase contrast in temperature and ensure 2 months' rest for the plant.

Saintpaulia (African violet)

QUITE DIFFICULT

These delicate plants, with their attractive, fleshy leaves and stems bearing small daisy-shaped flowers in mauves, pinks and white shades, have many admirers – and deservedly so. But be warned: they can be temperamental. When given the right (and difficult to achieve) balance of warmth, shade and moisture, they can bloom happily all year round.

The species was discovered in the Usambara mountains in South Africa by Baron St Paul St Claire in the late 1800s and was first grown commercially in America. It came originally from Tanzania, in a delicate deep-blue colour, and grew on steep and wind-swept rocks and in crevasses, its flowers up to 3cm/1in wide.

Saintpaulia has round, slightly hairy, heart-shaped leaves and there are variegated varieties, ones with serrated edges, crinkled edges or rolled edges. The flowers may be single, double, frilled, multi-coloured or star-shaped – the choice is endless . . . White African violets will revert to purple quite quickly.

In its native habitat *Saintpaulia* will last for a number of years – as it can as an indoor plant, though it is better kept a couple of years and then replaced with fresh flowering stock.

S. hybrida

'Fancy Pants'

S. Rhapsodie

CARE

Light and temperature
Warm conditions (16°C/60°F) help the plant to flourish. It likes adequate light, but no direct sun, as the leaves and flowers scorch easily.

Water and feeding
Always water from the bottom since water over the leaves and flowers will mark them. Stand in a saucer and fill twice weekly. After 30 minutes drain off the excess water. Use lukewarm water. Feed fortnightly during spring and summer with liquid houseplant fertilizer diluted to half strength.

Propagation
Can be grown from seed but the seedlings vary in quality. Much simpler are leaf cuttings. These root easily in a peat and sand mixture at about 20°C/68°F and will be in flower 6 months later. Rest the plant for 6–8 weeks at a lowish temperature, keeping it on the dry side every now and then. This helps to form flower buds and, when brought back into warmer temperatures with more water, will produce a flush of flowers.

Repotting
Only every second year and make sure the new container is only just bigger than the old one.

PROBLEMS

When leaves turn pale, the plant needs feeding or is receiving too much direct sun. Feed or move to a darker spot.

The plant needs repotting if there is more than a single crown or the leaves are small and too close together. You may limit flowering unless you separate out the crowns so that only 1 grows in the pot.

If the plant does not flower, but looks healthy, add a little superphosphate to the water. A lack of light is the most common cause of no flowers.

Mouldy leaves and flowers are caused by botrytis. Destroy affected leaves and spray with a systemic fungicide.

Whitefly and mealy bug should be treated with insecticide.

Rotting leaves and flowers are caused by too much water. Always water from below, and never overwater.

Some of the many Saintpaulia leaf types

Variegated   Serrated   Spoon-shaped   Lance-shaped

The most commonly-seen African violet

Senecio cruentis hybridus (Florists' cineraria)

QUITE EASY

This plant comes in almost every colour imaginable except yellow. It grows to 60cm/2ft and is covered with masses of small daisy-shaped flowers in early spring. There are dwarf, single and double varieties available, but the doubles are limited in their range of colours and will flower less freely. Buy plants with a few open flowers and plenty of buds; the flowering season lasts up to 2 months.

Senecio cruentis is very popular with parks departments for display purposes and is a good conservatory plant, preferring cool temperatures and little direct sun.

Its original habitat is the Canary Islands, where it grows as a half-hardy perennial, high up on the damp mountainsides in cool conditions. As a houseplant, it should be discarded after flowering.

Cineraria likes to have plenty of air circulation and humidity

Two of the many colour variations of singles | Double | Stellata

PROBLEMS

Yellow leaves are caused by draughty conditions. Move the plant to a more protected position.

Wilting leaves and drooping flowers are caused by the plant being either too dry and hot or overwatered. Resite the plant and reduce watering.

Flowers die prematurely if the plant is underwatered or receives too much sunlight.

CARE

Light and temperature.
Cinerarias like cool temperatures between 13°C/55°F. A north-facing windowsill is ideal. Keep out of direct sun, which will cause the plants to wilt and they will never recover completely.

Water and feeding
Water, then allow to dry out. Take care not to overwater and ensure good drainage. Feeding is not necessary as this only produces coarse plants with excessively sized leaves.

Propagation
From seed in summer, but earlier sowings will produce plants that bloom in midwinter. Do not bury the fine seed, but cover with glass or polythene. When the seedlings appear, spray them often, pot up in September and keep in an unheated greenhouse. When buds appear, raise the temperature to 13°C/55°F.

Repotting
Not necessary; plants are discarded after flowering.

Sinningia hybridus (Florist's gloxinia)

QUITE DIFFICULT

With its large bell-like flowers and luxuriant velvety leaves, *Gloxinia* is among the prettiest and most striking of flowering plants. The majority of varieties available now are hybrids, developed by nursery men from *Sinningia speciosa* crossed with *S. regina* way back in the early 1900s. Much of the work was done by a German botanist, Wilhelm Sinning, hence the genus name. From this, numerous other hybrids have been developed in almost every imaginable colour.

In its native habitat of southern Brazil it grows on damp, rocky slopes and has violet-blue flowers which face outwards rather than up. Modern hybrids have much larger flowers, which come into bloom from early spring to late summer. With proper care, they will remain in flower for up to 2 months. Gloxinias are tubers – they should only be purchased if plenty of flower buds are obvious and the leaves look glossy. They will do well as indoor plants for 2 or more years.

Never wet the leaves of the gloxinia

CARE

Light and temperature
Bright light, away from direct sunlight. Average warmth, with a minimum of 16°C/60°F throughout the flowering season. During winter months, keep at lower temperatures and move the plant back to the warmth in order to 'force' it into flowering.

Water and feeding
Keep the soil moist at all times while the plant is blooming. Water with soft, warm water and feed every fortnight with a weak solution of liquid fertilizer during the flowering season. Never allow the leaves to get wet. After flowering, reduce water and stop feeding. Allow to dry out when the leaves turn yellow and store the pot at 10°C/50°F.

Propagation
Take leaf cuttings in summer and pot in fresh compost at a constant temperature of 22°C/71°F or more. Artificial light is essential from late autumn to late winter for seeds sown in spring; not an easy task for the enthusiastic amateur.

Repotting
Wait for tubers to produce shoots in spring before repotting them. Then only repot firm tubers; those that feel at all soggy will not do well. Plant hollow side up with the top of the tuber level with the surface of the soil. Keep warm and on the dry side until leaves emerge, then grow on in a warm, bright and humid position.

PROBLEMS

If the plant collapses, it has been overwatered, or has poor drainage, or has been watered with cold instead of room-temperature water.

Hot dry air causes curled leaves with brown tips. Place the plant in a saucer of wet gravel to increase humidity and ensure that the plant does not get too much sun.

If the leaves become pale, place in a brighter position, but keep away from direct sunlight. Feed the plant more than usual.

The plant hates draughts and will droop if placed in an over-exposed position. Move to a warmer, more sympathetic place.

Gloxinia has one of the richest and most varied type of flower

Solanum (Winter cherry, false Jerusalem cherry)

EASY

Solanum capsicastrum has bright red berries for up to 6 months during wintertime

CARE

Light and temperature
Plenty of light, but not too warm – 13°C/55°F is ideal, with the maximum temperature 18°C/64°F. In summer place outdoors, as *Solanum* appreciates a good bake.

Water and feeding
Water very frequently while flowering and never let it dry out. Feed with weak solutions of liquid fertilizer every fortnight. Humidity is important; mist often and stand the plant on a tray of damp pebbles if possible.

Propagation
Sow seed in spring in a propagator at about 16°C/61°F. Stem-tip cuttings can also be attempted at this time.

Repotting
Repot when the plant outgrows its container, which could be several times in its first season. If kept for a second year, repot after pruning quite stringently in spring.

PROBLEMS

Grey mould can attack the plant. Spray with systemic fungicide.

If yellow rings appear on the leaves, destroy the plant. It is infected with tomato spotted wilt virus for which there is no cure. Spray with fertilizer containing magnesium if the lower leaves turn yellow with brown spots.

If the berries fall this is usually due to insufficient light. Move the plant to a south-facing windowsill.

The winter cherry, introduced from Brazil and Uruguay at the end of the seventeenth century, belongs to the potato family.

Solanum capsicastrum (the false Jerusalem cherry) produces fruit berries which ripen from green to red, yellow and orange. These berries are poisonous so keep well away from children. It is a popular plant usually bought in fruit around Christmas and lasts well indoors. Delicate but cheerful white flowers, similar to those of the potato, appear in June and July, but the berries are the more attractive feature. It can reach 30–38cm/12–15in high and will grow to that height from seed in one season.

Solanum pseudocapsicum is the true Jerusalem cherry. There is a pretty variegated form of *S. capsicastrum* available on occasions.

The plant can be kept for 2 Christmas seasons; thereafter it fruits less freely and should be discarded.

Spathiphyllum (Sail plant, peace lily)

QUITE EASY

Spathiphyllum wallisii, which originates in Colombia, is one of the best plants for indoor gardening as it is undemanding of light and care. It comes as no surprise to find that it is a member of the lily family and has exceptionally attractive leaves as well as flowers.

Its glossy bright green leaves lean out like sails from the centre, 30cm/12in high and 90cm/36in across. *Spathiphyllum* 'Mauna Loa' is bigger, growing to 1m/40in high and wide. This is probably a hybrid, bred from *Spathiphyllum floribunda* crossed with a Hawaiian hybrid developed in America. The flower head comprises a white spathe encompassing a 9cm/3in long spadix which is usually coloured white or pale green. For the first few days the flower has scent; thereafter this will fade but the flower should last for around 6 weeks. The plant itself should live for 10 years or more if not maltreated.

Spathiphyllum is a rhizome. It can grow enormously in a single season, doubling in size given the correct conditions. A most rewarding plant to grow.

CARE

Light and temperature
In summer, keep away from direct sun and maintain the temperature at 18–21°C/64–70°F. Research in Holland has shown that less light, rather than more, makes for more flowering. In winter, as much light as possible and keep at 16–18°C/60–64°F.

Water and feeding
This plant grows naturally in high humidity and warmth. With temperatures over 16°C/60°F, the leaves should be misted daily. Place the plant in a saucer filled with wet pebbles. Always keep the soil moist. Feed each fortnight while in flower.

Propagation
Offsets can be separated and planted into humus-rich compost. Seed can be grown but this is a demanding method for the amateur indoor gardener.

Repotting
When repotting divide large plants, in late spring, using humus-rich houseplant compost. New growth will be encouraged.

Remove the old flower stalks of *Spathiphyllum*, as they brown quickly

PROBLEMS

Red spider mite and greenfly can infest the plant. Spray with insecticide.

Floppy leaves indicate too little water. Immerse the pot in a bucket or sink and soak thoroughly, then drain well. Never allow the rootball to get soggy.

If the plant does not bloom, consider feeding and repot if potbound. Large plants can be divided.

If the leaves begin to yellow, the plant could be suffering from too much sunlight. Remove yellow leaves and place in a more shaded position.

Stephanotis floribunda

(Brides's flower, wax flower, Foradora jasmine, Madagascar jasmine)

DIFFICULT

This is a glorious climber when in flower during early summer, with its waxy white flowers much prized by florists for bridal bouquets.

Stephanotis is similar to the gardenia in that it hates changes of environment and temperature. It is ideal for a conservatory, where the white flowers hang down in bunches from the trailing stalks that can be left to climb or weave along a roof beam. However, it is often sold trained around hoops.

It comes from tropical Madagascar and was introduced into Europe in 1839. It can reach 6m/20ft or more, but if grown in a pot it should be kept compact by regular pruning. Plants may rest for several years and then suddenly burst into flower when there is sufficient light stimulus. A period of baking in sunlight helps this light-hungry plant enormously.

The *Stephanotis* has intoxicatingly scented flowers, usually in summertime

CARE

Light and temperature
It must be placed on a windowsill for light, but shielded from the midday sun. The ideal summer temperature is 15–21°C/60–70°F, with somewhat lower winter levels of 10°C/50°F

Water and feeding
Water frequently in summer but in winter just keep the compost from drying out. Use lime-free, warm water. Feed once a fortnight in summer and place the pot on wet gravel in a saucer, keeping the water level just below that of the pot. To induce humidity spray the leathery leaves, but never the flowers, at least once a week.

Propagation
For young plants growing at a great rate repot in good houseplant compost, perhaps as often as twice a year.

Repotting
Repot each spring. Cut back any straggly growth. After 5 years, replace the topsoil.

PROBLEMS

If the pot is moved or turned, the flower buds may drop so try to avoid handling the plant as much as possible.

Leaves will turn yellow if limey water is used. Make sure it is tepid and lime-free.

Red spider mite, scale insect and mealy bug often attack this plant. Spray each month with diluted malathion. Remove scale insect with methylated spirit swabs.

Streptocarpus (Cape primrose)

EASY

The delicate *Streptocarpus* or Cape primrose, which as its name suggests comes from subtropical Southern Africa, was brought to Europe in the 1820s. It grows naturally in humid, leafy shaded soil, often clinging to rocky surfaces, and can cope with semi-shaded conditions within the home.

Recently plant breeders have produced a range of hybrids. Purple or mauve is still the predominant colour, and 'Constant Nymph' the old favourite, but there are many different shades within this spectrum, from the deep purple of 'Amanda' to the soft mauve petals and darker throat stripes of 'Heidi'. White, pink and red varieties are also found.

Other varieties include the pretty mauve *Streptocarpus saxorum*, which can be trained into an attractive hanging plant, and the extraordinary *Streptocarpus wenlandii* with only one enormous leaf, that is red underneath.

The plant flowers twice a year and will live for 2 to 3 years before it needs replacing. After flowering cut the stems at the base to encourage new flower shoots. Mature plants grow to a height of 30cm/12in.

PROBLEMS

Streptocarpus is vulnerable to remarkably few pests and diseases. Give it the conditions outlined and it will thrive.

Shrivelled leaves suggest the plant is too dry. Increase watering.

Droopy leaves again indicate it is too dry. Increase watering.

Leaf stems may rot if the plant is too wet and too cold. Water less and move to a warmer place. Dusting with sulphur may help.

Prone to greenfly. These tend to attack the flower stems rather than the leaves or flowers themselves. Spray with insecticide. The stems may also be attacked by thrips; treat in the same way.

'Falling Stars'   'Stella'

'Heidi'   'Amanda'

CARE

Light and temperature
Streptocarpus is a remarkably tolerant plant in most respects, but it does need plenty of light. Protect it from direct sunlight in summer. The ideal temperature is 16–18°C/63–67°F.

Water and feeding
Water 2–3 times a week in summer, but do not let the plant stand in water. In centrally heated rooms, increase the humidity by placing the pot in damp pebbles. Good drainage is vital. It does not require much feeding – a half-strength dose once every two weeks is plenty.

Repotting
Repot every spring in peat-based compost into a pot one size up. *Streptocarpus* likes fresh soil even if it doesn't need more space, so replace the top 2.5cm/1in of soil.

Propagation
They are easy to propagate. Leaf cuttings should be taken in summer. Cut a leaf along the central vein, cover the cut with rooting hormone and plant the cut surface in sharp sand.

Zantedeschia (Calla lily, trumpet lily, arum lily)

QUITE EASY

This is an elegant plant from the Cape area of South Africa where it is known as the pig lily. There it grows from its tuber almost like a clump of weed in an area that is marshy through winter and dry in summer. It is a subtropical plant, able to tolerate quite differing day and night temperatures. *Zantedeschia* has broad arrow-shaped leaves up to 50cm/20in long and 20–25cm/10–12in wide on stems of up to 1m/3ft. Its flowers, which bloom in winter or early spring, are spectacular having a golden spadix circled by a velvety white spathe.

Z. aethiopica (arum lily), the most commonly seen, has the white spathe; *Z. rehmannii* (pink calla), from Natal, has leaves spotted with silvery white and in summer produces a delicate pink spathe; *Z. elliottiana* (golden calla) from the Transkei region has a rich deep yellow spathe in late spring to summer.

Provided callas are given a 2-month period of dormancy, when the leaves will die down, the plants can go on for many years.

Z. rehmannii

CARE

Light and temperature
In summer, the rhizome should be kept outside in the sun until late autumn. In October, bring it inside and keep in bright light at reasonably low temperatures. When growth starts, keep at 10–14°C/50–57°F for 3 months, then increase the temperature to over 16°C/61°F.

Water and feeding
Keep the rhizome dry in the summer dormancy period. In winter, water little at first, increasing as growth begins. During full growth keep the soil moist and place the pot in a bowl of water. Feed with liquid fertilizer each fortnight before flowering and weekly when in flower; thereafter cease feeding. Humidity is a natural demand of the calla during the flowering season so place over a tray of moist pebbles.

Propagation
Divide the rhizomes in autumn, keeping at least 1 shoot on each portion. Offsets can be removed and potted on.

Repotting
Each autumn, in humus-rich compost. There are often up to 3 or more rhizomes in a pot for effect.

PROBLEMS

Spray scale insects with insecticide, if infested.

Aphids and red spider mite will attack if conditions are too hot and dry. Treat and increase humidity.

Zantedeschia aethiopica, the arum lily

Index